Seven Deep Insecurities Men Don't Want Women to Know

STORIES OF MEN WHO SHARE

SHERI E RAGLAND

WESTBOW°
PRESS
A DIVISION OF THOMAS NELSON
& ZONDERVAN

Scripture quotations are from The Holy Bible, English Standard Version® (ESV®), copyright © 2001 by Crossway, a publishing ministry of Good News Publishers. Used by permission. All rights reserved.

Scripture taken from the King James Version of the Bible.

WestBow Press books may be ordered through booksellers or by contacting:

WestBow Press
A Division of Thomas Nelson & Zondervan
1663 Liberty Drive
Bloomington, IN 47403
www.westbowpress.com
1 (866) 928-1240

ISBN: 978-1-4908-9745-5 (sc)
ISBN: 978-1-4908-9747-9 (hc)
ISBN: 978-1-4908-9746-2 (e)

Library of Congress Control Number: 2015913763

Print information available on the last page.

WestBow Press rev. date: 08/07/2015

CONTENTS

Contents

To couples seeking positive relationships or marriages grounded in the promises of God, love, commitment, respect, equality, patience, and faith.

Love is patient and kind; love does not envy or boast; it is not arrogant or rude. It does not insist on its own way; it is not irritable or resentful;[1] it does not rejoice at wrongdoing, but rejoices with the truth. Love bears all things, believes all things, hopes all things, endures all things. Love never ends.
—1 Corinthians 13:4–8 English Standard Version

---

[1] resentful: "does not count up wrongdoing."

PREFACE

I thank God for this book project. He has given me a simple yet beautiful idea that has evolved into a fun and inspiring project I believe will help people with their marriages and relationships and add value to society. God's wisdom has guided me successfully through every step of this project.

I am grateful for the support I have received from resources and a professional community that has provided me with successful strategies for addressing relationship challenges with individuals and couples of all ages, cultures, and socioeconomic backgrounds. However, further discussion needs to occur between individuals and couples on gender-specific topics of relationships that have not been openly discussed, such as men and their insecurities.

I thank my friends and colleagues for their contributions to this project; I could not have accomplished it without them.

As a result of this project, I have recognized that relationships are to be treasured, celebrated, and nurtured as beautiful gifts from God that can provide joy, peace, stability, companionship, respect, patience, and everlasting love that should never be taken for granted.

INTRODUCTION

Dating, love, intimacy, romance, communicating, and trust are relationship topics that support multibillion-dollar professions and industries such as psychology, psychiatry, religion, food and entertainment, fashion, retail, and travel as well as social media. Even though couples have invested $50 billion a year on weddings (State of Our Unions 2012, 1), they have spent far less on premarital counseling to protect their marriage (Ottney 2013). Couples who have spent $75 to $150 per hour for twelve or more marriage counseling sessions had a success rate of approximately 55 percent (Elichmann 2014, 1).

In spite of marriage counseling, nearly one million couples a year experience divorce (CDC 2011). If couples invest time and money in relationships, why do they continue to have the same difficulties? Common issues that many couples experience are poor communications (Elichmann 2014; Horan 2013; Shimberg 1999; Sorgen 2012); sex, money, trust, lack of appreciation, unforgiveness, expectations, and technology (McGuinness 2013) and more-complex issues that are multidimensional as well as linear. As a result, relationships are dynamic (Courtright, Millar, Rogers, and Bagarozzi 1990). For couples who did seek professional help, it was often too late to save the marriage because the damage had been done by year six of the marriage (Horan 2013). An average of 55 percent of couples who had received marriage counseling saw their issues resurface and deteriorate the relationship (Marriage Guardian 2014, 1).

Recently, governments have increased their involvement in the marriage business to proactively increase the success rate of couples. In July of 2014, the Australian Government launched a campaign to provide vouchers worth $200 to over 100,000 newlyweds for marriage counseling as an intervention measure for couples (Chalmers 2014). Additionally, state governments may use incentives to ensure that couples take every measure to live in a satisfying marriage. For instance, states such as Maryland and Michigan may consider expediting the marriage license process, if couples obtain pre-marriage counseling, while Iowa may consider offering couples a tax-break (Stanley & Markman 2014, 1). Such laws may cause couples to think about taking proactive measures to protect their marriage.

Relationships are further complicated by the evolving roles of males and females in today's society and external factors such as technology and feminism (Gilbert 2009). Couples also bring unrealistic expectations, negative thinking, and set behaviors to their relationships; they lack the appropriate support and resources to address relationship challenges (Temple 2009) and often the insight and wisdom to resolve them. The reasons why are not limited to those mentioned, but they are central to our chapter findings and discussions.

Focusing on a gender-specific topic provides additional insight into the existing body of information on relationships. I investigate relationship topics through discussions with male colleagues, friends, and individuals on subjects men rarely discuss, such as their deep-seated insecurities. As a result of an investigation, I have discovered that men discuss their insecurities among themselves but not with their partners; this book focuses on seven top insecurities that were identified by men who took part in this study.

In chapter 1 of part 1, Robert Harris described his journey of self-discovery beginning with the memories of his childhood in Memphis, Tennessee. He reflected on the simplicity of his life and family togetherness. However, the harsh reality of poverty challenged his simple world with the complexity of surviving in the "ghetto." In chapter 2, he provided personal insecurities that plagued friendships in his teenage years and ultimately his adult relationships. Robert described his emotional struggle with negative thinking, pride, anger, low self-esteem, control, and aggression as a teenager.

In chapter 3, he identified failed friendships and relationships as the consequences of his negative behaviors and emotions that stemmed from his mother's abuse and control.

In chapter 4, Robert revealed how he confronted those insecurities and became a better person in general and in relationships.

His memoir provides a true experience of a man willing to share his past challenges of manhood as well as the changed man he is today because of his faith in Jesus Christ. It provides a foundation for part 2: Seven Deep Insecurities of Men, which speaks to the insecurities men like Robert experience but do not discuss with the women in their lives.

In part 2: Seven Deep Insecurities of Men, chapters 1 through 7 identify what men perceive to be the top insecurities that affect relationships, beginning with the most to the least important. In part 3—Reflections, chapter 1 provides strategies for addressing insecurities, such as using open communications with partner; taking a holistic approach that considers the emotional, physical, and spiritual aspects of people; creating a stable environment; and taking advantage of resources. The conclusion is a summary of the findings and includes a quick list of ten items that men can do to better themselves and promote a healthy relationship with their partners or spouses.

This book suggests successful strategies for addressing those insecurities and inspiring healthy dialogue among men and women as well as couples of all cultural backgrounds regarding male insecurities that could negatively affect relationships.

Part 1 serves as the foundation for obtaining feedback from men who identify their top insecurities in part 2, while part 3 offers reflections and highlights the perceptions of men about their insecurities and strategies to address them. The conclusion summarizes the importance of the findings for discussion and resolution.

PART I

Robert Harris's Memoir: Journey to Manhood

Sweet Childhood Memories in Memphis

Robert Harris was born at John Gaston Hospital on August 19, 1961, in Memphis, Tennessee. He lived on Driving Park Court, a one-way street in North Memphis lined with wooden shotgun houses, narrow shacks of three rooms with crevices in the walls, floors, and ceilings. The neighborhood consisted predominately of large black families. On a normal day, neighborhood children ran out of their tiny houses and filled the streets with laughter and playing.

All of these shotgun houses had few windows, one tiny bathroom with no tub, and no insulation. During the winters, one stove tried to heat any one house and counteract the winter air blowing through the cracks. When the front and back doors were open, anyone standing on the porch or at the back could see straight through the houses. For the Harris family, it was modest living at best.

Robert had one brother and three sisters; he was the middle child who always wanted to be the center of attention. His father left the family when they were children and led a separate life. He didn't provide any support to the family of six and rarely saw his children. The Harris family was so poor that each member had only a few clothes to wear. Their monthly welfare assistance barely covered the food and the bare essentials for the six of them. Robert and his siblings were always excited when his mother received food stamps; that meant they would get ham, lettuce, and tomato sandwiches but no cheese—cheese was a luxury. Strawberries and milk constituted their dessert.

When the food stamps ran out, they sometimes ate raw potatoes or carrots. At times, they were so hungry that they made sandwiches based solely on what was in the kitchen; ketchup and sugar or mayonnaise sandwiches at times filled their little bellies but of course barely curbed their appetites.

His mother didn't have a full-time job. She cooked and sold barbeque ribs, pies, and cakes to neighbors to make extra money. Those were sweet treats for the Harris kids whenever there were leftovers, but that wasn't very often.

Christmas: A Feast for a King

Christmas for the Harris family was very simple; they didn't put up trees and sometimes received no gifts. Robert remembers one such giftless Christmas because his mother simply didn't have the money. He was sad and disappointed because his friends had received gifts from their parents.

However, good food was a sweet distraction to Robert; that made up a bit for not receiving gifts. The Harris family Christmas dinners consisted of ham, candied yams, sweet potato pies, cakes, spaghetti and meatballs, collard greens, nuts, and peppermint sticks. Robert remembers that as nothing short of a feast, and he and his siblings played with their friends and the toys they received and got lost in the excitement of sharing.

In short, Robert's childhood was simple; he enjoyed hearty meals when the family could afford them. When food wasn't on his mind, he was a normal boy filled with wonder and excitement and a desire to explore all life.

Curious and Hardheaded

Young Robert got in trouble more than he should have trying to satisfy his curiosity. Once, he asked his mother if he could play in the yard for a little while; she let him, but she warned him not to go past the front yard. He was stubborn, however, and decided not to obey her. He received a whipping he still remembers, and that one wasn't his first or last.

After a while, whippings were just threats his mother followed through with. They were no longer a deterrent to

Robert; he often ignored the warnings and simply suffered the consequences. He did what he wanted to.

On another occasion, he and two friends decided to play in a large field behind a row of houses near some railroad tracks. A hardwood site by the tracks looked abandoned, but it was just closed for the weekend. The site had a large warehouse with a lumber yard and tractors. The setting intrigued him, especially because of the haunted stories his mother and aunt used to tell his brother, sisters, and him. He saw rats the size of cats that would creep from the fields and into the house at night. His mother told him never to play around the tracks or he would get in trouble. Like many other kids, he ignored her warnings and explored.

One day, Robert and his friends decided to play in the field near the railroad tracks. As they played, they moved deeper into the field. They climbed up and down the trains cars and had so much fun they didn't pay any attention to the time. It was getting dark, and he knew his mother was looking for him. They sprinted past the tracks, through the field, and finally reached their neighborhood.

Some kids who lived close by warned him his mother was on the prowl. Robert could feel the butterflies in his stomach as he swiftly ran to his house; he knew he was in trouble. When he reached the house, his mother said, "I thought I told you to stay in the front yard. Fetch a switch from the tree in the backyard."

He knew he was about to get a whipping with that all-natural substance called a switch about two to three feet long and about a quarter-inch in diameter. Robert had to fetch his own switch; if the switch was too small, his mother made him get another. At times, she made him tie

6

two switches together for more stability, and the pain they inflicted was great.

The more he was whipped, the angrier he became. He rebelled against his mother's abuse every chance he got. He made it a habit to do exactly what she asked him not to do to express his resentment toward her control and abuse. Anyone who questioned or challenged him became an immediate target. His rebellious attitude, however, provided him with the attitude and ability to survive the life of broken homes, violence, and poverty in the projects, where they moved.

The Scutterfield Projects: Luxury Apartments

Robert was six when he moved with his family to Henry Oaks Manor projects known as Scutterfield to those living in North Memphis. Scutterfield consisted of low-income apartments often called the ghetto. However, the Harris family thought their apartment was luxurious compared to where they used to live. They had two large bedrooms and a storage room that was half the size of one of the bedrooms. Robert and his brother shared the storage room, his sisters slept in one of the large bedrooms, and his mother slept in the other. Robert and his brother no longer had to share a room with their sisters. Robert happily stated, "We have privacy at last."

The Harris kids were new in the neighborhood, and the other kids wanted to know who they were. Robert took notice of the surroundings and saw some attractive girls he wanted to get to know. They wanted to get to know him too.

He had his eye on Keri, an attractive girl; they were both very interested in getting to know each other. James, a guy who had a crush on Keri, was upset when she paid attention to Robert. As a result, when the neighborhood kids got together for fun and games, James played a little rougher than necessary with Robert, which caused Robert to confront James about his aggression. James became defensive, frowned at Robert, and never said a word.

One of James's friends told Robert that James wanted to fight him. Robert said, "No problem." Robert was small, but he could defend himself very well and was always ready for a fight. So they fought. James lunged at Robert and got the shock of his life; Robert positioned himself underneath James, lifted him up, and slammed him to the ground. "Wow!" was all the kids watching could say.

Robert was on top of James, punching him in the face and roughing him up a little. After the fight, which was the talk of the neighborhood for a week, Robert gained respect from the neighborhood kids and didn't worry about anyone underestimating him. He also received special attention from Keri, and James never bothered him again. Robert's mother, however, heard about the fight and was concerned that it might create tension between neighborhood kids and the Harrises, especially because they were new in the neighborhood.

The Harris sons and daughters stuck together no matter what; they shared a very tight bond. If one had a problem with a neighborhood kid, the others would back him or her up. They were individuals at home, but outside, everyone had to deal with the entire Harris group, not just one.

School Days

Robert thought it was cool that he was going to school with the neighborhood kids. After school, he would meet his friends in the park and share stories about the school day. They talked about their teachers, girls, and having fun.

When Robert got home from school, his mother was excited to hear about his first day at the new school and what had taken place in class. He told her about all the fun games he played, the friends he met, and how he couldn't wait to go back the next day. However, there were times when school days weren't so fun because of encounters with bullies.

The Bullying Stops with Him

Robert also had to learn the hard facts about life in the projects. He said, "Respect didn't come easy. It had to be earned. I had to fight for my beliefs and not let anyone take advantage of me because there were plenty of bullies in the projects where we lived." For a while, he was constantly in fights because he refused to be bullied and wanted respect, which could mean fighting everyone in the neighborhood his age. Robert won all but two of his fights; he earned respect and acquired many friends. He also received attention from the neighborhood girls. In his mind, he was the man.

Bullies were everywhere, even in school. The first time Robert fought a bully in school, he was suspended. Robert knew if his mother found out, he would be in deep trouble. His teacher wrote a letter to his mother to let her know that he had been bullied and had defended himself, which was the right thing to do. His teacher said she was proud of him because he had refused to let other kids take advantage of him.

Robert was never bullied again after he returned to school. He never saw the bully he had beaten up again. He assumed that the bully had transferred or dropped out. Robert's uncles heard about the fight and joked about it; they took credit for having taught him how to fight. Robert's mother didn't like her brothers teaching him how to fight because she taught the Harris kids to respect others, especially elders.

Spare the Rod and Spoil the Child

When Robert was growing up, fighting was considered bad behavior that warranted whippings. Robert was taught that if you behaved badly in school, your teacher punished you by making you stand in a corner the whole day and writing a note to your parents for misbehaving. For the Harris kids, the fear of getting in trouble with their mother when they got home was greater than the punishment they received at school. Robert said, "If you were five minutes late for school, the teacher sent you to the principal's office, and you got five licks on your hand or on your bottom with a paddle or a razor strap." But they would then face more discipline at home. Robert said, "Kids weren't as disrespectful when I was growing up. Disrespect warranted punishment that made them think twice about doing it again. The lack of discipline has created a generation of young people who have little regard for the authority, adults, and others. And they're quick to react defensively about any little thing. Young men today address their frustrations through violence, crimes, gangs, drugs, and more."

Education and getting jobs are not priorities for young African-American men as can be seen from their high rate of dropping out of high school, according to the Department of Education. Robert said, "Parents can't even discipline their children with a whipping because it's illegal."

The Center for Disease Control (2004) attributes the top three causes of death among African-American men between ages eighteen and twenty-four to homicide, accidental injuries, and suicide. Robert feels we are losing our kids at very young ages to gang-related crimes. Today's youth are different from what they were when he grew up. He stated, "When I think about who I am today, I don't feel bad about many of those whippings because they saved my life. I thank God for my mother and how she taught us to respect others no matter what."

Proverbs 13:24 (KJV) tells us, "Spare the rod and spoil the child." Robert's mother lived by this Scripture. Robert said, "I'm not sure how it applied to me, because I certainly wasn't spoiled. I had to fight to defend and protect myself. Little did I know that the force and aggression I experienced began to define my personality at a very young age. For me, violence was a means of survival in the projects. My personal struggle was a mere reflection of the civil disobedience that manifested in Memphis and the South during the 1960s."

Sheri E Ragland

The Death of Dr. Martin Luther King: Black Mondays

The segregation between whites and blacks in the South became even more apparent after the death of Dr. Martin Luther King. Robert remembers little about Dr. King, except for what he learned in school, museums, books, magazines, movies, and word of mouth. He stated, "I vaguely remember his death at the Lorraine Hotel in Memphis on April 4, 1968. However, I do remember the racial tension that occurred in Memphis after his death."

Over a year after the death of Dr. King, racial tension was at an all-time high in Memphis. Protests and riots led by the black community led to "Black Mondays." On a Monday in October 1969, black students were let out of school early to unite with adults in marching against discrimination. The NAACP was a leading force in in promoting equality through a highly organized campaign that boycotted white businesses. The NAACP also encouraged marches that included black students, parents, families, workers, and teachers. "Black Mondays," as they were called, lasted for nearly two months. During that time, Robert's mother made his brother and sisters come straight home from school on Mondays. Curfews kept blacks off the streets in Memphis. Robert remembers that no black person was allowed to walk or drive in Memphis after dusk. Robert said, "If we were caught on the streets after the curfew, the National Guard sprayed us with tear gas." There was always one brave or not-so-wise individual who felt the curfew could be ignored.

James, a young black man in his twenties, lived on the second floor of the apartment complex where Robert and his family lived. On one Black Monday, James walked around the projects after curfew; a member of the National Guard sprayed tear gas on the back of his neck. He ran to his apartment crying like a baby because it burned and hurt very much. James said that jail was a better option than the pain. This was the first time Robert had ever seen a grown man cry. Robert's mother tried to help James by placing a wet towel on his neck. James swore and yelled because of the pain and said he was going to get the National Guard for what they had done to him.

James and Robert's mother thought they would get revenge by throwing bottles in the streets to flatten the tires of the National Guard's jeeps when they drove down the street. The attack began at dusk. Robert was excited when his mom let him throw a bottle, but he was disappointed that he couldn't throw one all the way into the street, however.

During the curfew, people stood outside of the apartment complexes as if they were watching a parade. It was unusual to see the National Guard driving down our street in their jeeps as if we were the problem. Robert used to watch them from the window as they patrolled the streets in two or three jeeps at a time with rifles strapped to their backs, ready to attack anyone who disobeyed the curfew.

As a child, Robert found it hard to understand the depth of the racism in Memphis; all he knew was that something was wrong because his simple life of pleasure had been interrupted with little explanation other than what he saw. Even though Black Mondays lasted only two months, it felt like eternity to a child who had more important things to do, such as have fun.

Fun and Games at Eight

When he was eight, Robert wanted a little more freedom. He asked his mother if he could join day camp, which would give him the opportunity to travel to places he had never been, such as Shiloh, Tennessee, where the Civil War battle took place on April 6, 1862. While waiting for his mother to answer, Robert told her about Ulysses S. Grant and how he led Union soldiers to a victory over the Confederates. Robert also told his mother that the battle led to 23,000 casualties; and, was considered to be the "bloodiest" battle in American history during the Civil War. Without further delay, Robert's mother said, "Yes."

Robert was so excited about going that he didn't think much about not having shoes. On the day of the trip, a shoeless Robert boarded the bus. No matter how much he tried to hide them under the seat, everyone stared at his bare feet and whispered to each other. Robert stared back and tried not to think about the insulting remarks. His desire to make the trip was much greater than his embarrassment about not having shoes. He was the center of attention for a while, but the other kids got used to the fact that he had no shoes and once again acted normally, talking, and playing. Once they reached their destination, all the kids except Robert played kick ball; he just sat back and watched. It ended up being a fun day because the attention had been on him for a while.

One day, Robert's mother called him in from playing to eat dinner. He told her he wasn't ready to eat. She insisted that he eat before his food got cold, and Robert reluctantly obeyed, but he was angry because dinner had interrupted his playing. All he wanted to do was play simple games such as kick ball, dodge ball, cowboys and Indians, red light green light, and hide-and-seek. Robert said, "Today, I rarely see kids playing those games because of the infusion of tech toys in their lives at a very early age. Kids today are missing out on simple fun and games. Cell phones, computers, and digital toys take the place of climbing trees, riding bikes, flying kites, playing tag games, and making tents and houses out of cardboard."

Memphis summers were long and hot. On summer nights, whenever his mother allowed them to, Robert, his brother, and their sisters would head outside to watch the stars. They would lie in the grass and count as many as they could. The first to spy the Big and Little Dippers shouted their names out.

One of Robert's adventure sites was a lumber yard a couple of blocks away, where he got two-by-fours with which he made stilts. He practiced every day for a week until he could walk on them with ease. He would pretend to be a giant who was racing. Another time, he put his imagination to work and became an instant cowboy, using a mop as a horse and his hand for a pistol. He once bought a kite for ten cents and made a tail for it out of his mother's old stockings. His imagination knew few boundaries; being young and poor never stopped him from being adventurous.

His happy childhood days make him think of the good life God intended children to have and sweet family times. The Harris family was content with basic necessities such as food, clothing, and a roof over our heads, and that was good enough for Robert then.

Got a Job at Age Ten

The corner store was a shotgun house that carried basic household items and things that most kids wanted to play with or eat. In those days, a penny could buy a cookie with cream filling, and ten cents would buy an ice cream cone. Whenever Robert had a dime or more, he shared it with his brother, sisters, and friends. He was the kid with all the snacks. As a result, the neighborhood kids always wanted to play with him.

During the summer, Robert's mother allowed him to work with a family friend who sold watermelons; on a good day, Robert made as much as three dollars, a fortune for a ten-year-old. Robert was so excited about the money he made, and his mother taught him how to start saving. Though saving made him unhappy—he wanted to buy snacks to share with his brother and sisters—his mother had the final word.

Robert was always looking for ways to make more money. At age twelve, he found a job on a truck selling eggs in the neighborhood and made enough money to buy snacks for friends and family as well as save. He didn't have much, but whatever he earned, he shared with family and friends.

Waiting Up for His Mother

Robert's mother stayed out until the early morning hours. During the week, she hung out until two or three in the morning. He didn't like it when she stayed out late because he didn't sleep well until she was safely home. When she came home, the lights were out, and he could see only her shadow outside. The big wig she wore made her look scary. He knew it was her when she spoke and the way she opened the door. She rattled the doorknob, as did the rest of the family; it was their way of announcing that a family member was entering. Robert would be happy to see his mother and would hug her, relieved she had come home safe. She would laugh when Robert squeezed her. Robert would ask, "Why did you stay out so late?" He never got an answer that made sense, but he was happy to see her. She always made him go to bed right away because she didn't feel like talking in the wee hours of the morning.

CHAPTER TWO

His Teenage Years and the Beginning of Anger

The Harris family didn't have much, but Robert's mother made sure the family was taken care of and always had something if not enough to eat. There were times when peanut butter and jelly sandwiches were all they had to eat until the next food stamps came in. Robert's mother often took them grocery shopping when they were very hungry, and the kids would eat grapes when their mother wasn't looking. Robert remembers that once, a nosey shopper told Robert's mother that they were eating grapes. "She lined us up like the three stooges and popped each one of us on the forehead. She told us not to touch anything and to wait until we got home to eat."

While living in the projects, the Harris family was placed on a waiting list to move into a larger apartment, when one became available. Three years later they moved into a two-story, three-bedroom apartment. One night, when the lights were out and everyone was supposedly asleep, Robert snuck downstairs to make a peanut butter and jelly sandwich though his mother had told him to drink water to fill up the empty spot if he was hungry. Unbeknownst to Robert, his sister was right behind him. She quietly hid in the front room until he finished eating. When he was on his way back to bed, she jumped out and startled him so much that he accidentally pushed her into their mother's glass lamp on the end table. The lamp fell; the crash woke his mother, who thought someone had broken in until she heard Robert and his sister blaming each other. She went downstairs, leather strap in hand, and started hitting the two culprits. Each time his mother swung at him, he pushed his sister in front of him, and she did the same with Robert. It became so funny that Robert's mother started laughing, grew tired of swinging the belt, and sent them to bed. All that running around and yelling had made him hungry again, but instead of eating more, Robert and his sister cleaned up the broken lamp before going to bed.

New Beginnings: Starting School

When Robert's older sisters were in high school, they were always excited about telling the family what they had learned in school. Their excitement was contagious; Robert was excited about the prospect of high school, but he was also nervous because he didn't know what to expect.

Once he got to school, however, he forgot his nervousness. He played and had fun with the other kids. After school, his older sister picked him up in front of the school and walked him home. Every day she asked him how school was, and he would report that he had had a great time. His mother would ask him about homework, but Robert did his homework in class; the only time he had homework was when the class didn't do well on a test.

When he was fourteen, Robert weighed only sixty-five pounds. His big afro made his head look bigger than his small fame. He was so skinny that he wore two pairs of pants to make himself look larger from the waist down. His mother could afford only three-dollar sneakers from the General Dollar Store. Robert remembered that their soles were so hard that they sounded like regular shoes. He was so active that the sneakers would start ripping apart in a week. Though his mother thought he was too rough on the sneakers, the shoes weren't made to last, especially on the feet of an active boy. Robert's mother told him to wear his torn sneakers until she was able to by him another pair, but he was too embarrassed to do that; the smell of athlete's feet seeped through the tears in his sneakers and traumatized everyone around him.

Robert remembered sitting in his fourth grade classroom years earlier and hearing the kids around him complain about a foul odor. "What's the problem?" the teacher asked. "Something stinks over here," the kids said. Robert knew they were talking about his feet, but he played along and acted as if he didn't know the cause. He was so embarrassed that he couldn't wait to get home and wash his feet.

Robert and his brother loved to play basketball. Each time he stopped to take a jump shot, his brother would call traveling on him because Robert's sneakers made him slip. They argued in spite of the fact they both knew the sneakers were the real issue.

When they did see eye to eye, they would talk about making enough to buy all the things they wanted. Both vowed to take care of their mother and the rest of the family because they all needed help beyond their means.

When the streetlights came on, his mother would call each of her children by name. At times, they got to stay out a little longer when their mother turned on the front porch light and watched them play. But after that, he had to be in the house to take a bath. Few families had showers in those days; that was a luxury beyond the means of most black families. If the Harris family didn't have soap, they used washing powder, which was hard on the skin. Robert remembers his body feeling like a shriveled-up prune. Since the family didn't have lotion, Robert would slap cooking grease on his skin to soothe the dryness. At night, however, mosquitoes and roaches would attack him as if he were a great meal. Summer was the worst time; flying bugs followed Robert around as if they were best buddies. And during the day, the sun baked his skin with extra heat. Eventually, he told his mother about the bugs. She laughed and said, "Don't use the grease."

The Beginning of Anger

During Robert's teenage years, Robert's mother forced him to go to church three to four times a week, but he rebelled against that because they had not gone to church that frequently in the past. Robert felt she was forcing him to become someone he didn't want to be. Furthermore, he didn't know anything about salvation. Without warning or explanation, his mother made him stop doing some of the fun things he loved such as listening to music, dancing, and hanging out with his friends. In his mind, it was just harmless fun all teenagers engaged in.

He also had to fast and pray without much preparation; going without food and water didn't make sense to him, and it would make him physically weak. His metabolism was high, he was very active, so, as a growing teenager, he was always hungry. As he grew older, he saw that his mother just wanted the best for him, but when he was younger, he couldn't understand why his mother had suddenly put the brakes on his life, which wasn't causing anyone any harm.

She, however, knew that teenagers were vulnerable on the streets based on her experience. She wanted to control his every move to make sure he didn't become a victim of the streets, but he resisted her efforts to curb his freedom. He let his rebellion and anger rule; he wanted to be a normal teenager who wanted to have fun; he wasn't interested in indulging in the bad side of the ghetto.

His mother was never the same once she became very religious. He could never understand the change and why she forced his brother and sisters to follow suit. There was nothing fun about his mother's choice to be religious. The Harris kids felt that they were always under the gun living in her house because she was very strict.

Robert's mother kept whipping him with a switch whenever he rebelled against her. He never felt he deserved such treatment, and once the pain wore off, his rebellious and curious ways kicked in once again.

Robert frequently spoke his mind during his teenage years. He felt he had the right to make some of his own choices about things he wanted to do, such as hang out with friends and attend events instead of going to church. He also wanted to keep the little money he earned instead of handing it over to his mother to buy sheets, pillowcases, or curtains. He often wanted to buy shoes, shirts, or slacks for himself. Robert's teenage years of fun were becoming filled with responsibilities.

When he was hanging out with friends and wasn't home at a certain time, his mother sent his brother or one of his sisters to look for him. He was summoned to go home to do chores such as cleaning his bedroom or taking out the garbage. His mother had no tolerance for any of Robert's excuses. He used to get whippings even as a teenager, and they would make him angry enough to fight his mother.

His anger began to rule him more and more as he desperately tried to cope with his mother's attempt to control his every move. The tension between Robert and his mother grew worse. During that time, it wasn't good for either of them to live under the same roof, especially because of the thoughts that went through his head that were anything but good.

Robert's bad behavior also surfaced in the classroom. Robert's teacher called his mother one day about his attitude; he was interrupting her class while she taught. As a result, his mother whipped him in front of the class. He was embarrassed and full of anger. To make matters worse, his class made fun of him for a while after the classroom incident. He was temperamental and ready to fight anyone who said anything to him. His sister told him that one of the kids had made fun of his mother. That was enough to provoke his temper. Robert found the kid, told him to never talk about his mother again, and broke his jaw.

Whippings: A Form of Control

Robert was deeply hurt and embarrassed by his mother's attempts to control him through whippings and curtailing his freedom. His hurt and sadness were replaced with hardness. The more she disciplined him, the angrier he became. He received so many whippings that he considered them to be abuse. He could do nothing about them, so rebellion became his outlet and led to the dominating and controlling behaviors he demonstrated as an adult.

His mother didn't understand why he behaved the way he did. The discipline she handed out was a family tradition meant to instill fear and control; she had learned this from her father and thought it was the best way to help her children make better choices. But his mother's strict ways made it difficult for Robert to manage his emotions in a healthy manner. As a result, he had a difficult time expressing himself, especially to girls. His attitude inspired him to find ways to make money to help supplement his family's income, but those ways were limited in the ghetto.

Hustling in the Ghetto

Robert worked part-time jobs during summers to help his mother pay bills and buy food. The money helped, but it wasn't enough for a family of six, especially without his father's assistance. He started selling marijuana to earn more. In the projects, people were poor, but plenty found enough money to buy marijuana. Robert was selling marijuana while living at home with his family. He liked the extra money he made, but it required him to work in the evenings, when people were available. He would always have to make up excuses for why he would miss the curfew his mother had set for him. His rebellion created tension between him and his mother. Eventually, she couldn't take his disobedience any longer. She gave him two options: join the army or go live with his father. Robert opted to move in with his father so he could continue to sell marijuana to help his family. His father didn't question his whereabouts as his mother had.

CHAPTER THREE

The Beginning of Manhood and His Controlling Behavior

Robert found staying with his father to be a sweet relief because he was free from his mother's overbearing ways. His mother didn't want to deal with his attitude anymore, and he didn't want to deal with hers. His father was never controlling or abusive. Living with him allowed Robert to be a normal teenager and indulge in bad behavior. His father was rarely home, and he offered little guidance when he was to a young man in need of it.

Robert's mother had never said anything positive about his father; she had made him sound like the worst human being on earth. After living with him for some time, Robert didn't understand why she was so bitter toward him. He didn't see his father as a worthless man but a troubled one with little direction and the proper support to deal with his alcoholism, a disease that later robbed him of his life. Robert and his father needed each other at that time, and they were excited about the opportunity to bond.

Bonding started with driving lessons. Robert's father taught him how to drive at a very young age in a schoolyard. At the time, he was only about five feet tall; his feet could hardly touch the gas pedal. He was so short that only the top of his head could be seen. Nonetheless, he learned how to drive very quickly. He would stop the car and raise his head and shout out, "What's up?" to people he knew.

He asked his father to take him to his neighborhood so his friends could see him drive. As he drove, he heard people saying, "That's Robert Harris driving that car." Robert glanced over at his father and could sense that he was proud of him.

Getting Caught: The Marijuana Hustle Ends

Robert's father worked as a truck driver for Kimberly-Clark Corporation in North Memphis. His father delivered products from the distribution center to store warehouses and sites Mondays through Fridays. Although the North Memphis site closed in 1994, Kimberly-Clark is a multi-billion dollar business operating in over 150 countries and is best known for Kleenex, Kotex, Huggies, Poise, and Depends products. His father liked to frequent the bars for drinks after work. Robert often drove his father to keep him from driving drunk. When Robert wasn't driving his father from bar to bar, he sold marijuana. Selling marijuana brought Robert good money quickly. The thrill of fast money ended when he was arrested for possession with intent to sell. Robert was a scared teenager behind bars for the first time; he didn't know what to expect. His father bailed him out, though he was very upset even though Robert was embarrassed. Robert didn't dwell on his setback because of guilt; his father had not been there for him when he was growing up, and his father knew that. He thought his father was going to send him back to his mother's house, but he didn't. Robert waited until things calmed down with his father. He also discovered another hustle.

Women: The Name of the Game

Robert had a clientele at bars around town for the marijuana he sold. His arrest helped him earn respect on the streets. He began to hang out at bars and poolrooms because he was interested in hustling on a higher level. The pimps he ran across were stylish dressers with tailor-made suits, alligator or Italian leather shoes, jewelry on their fingers, and big hats that set them apart. Their style and power were very attractive to a young man looking for a way to make more money.

More than anything else, Robert loved the Cadillacs they drove; those were signs of status and success. He also noticed they were some of the smoothest talkers he had ever heard. He did his best to discreetly listen to their conversations as he admired the beautiful women in fine clothes and shoes who always surrounded them. They were manicured from head to toe, and they would turn heads every time they walked into a bar or poolroom.

He was excited when the hookers paid attention to him. The slogan in the bar was, "The game is to be sold and not to be told." He was infatuated with the game of a pimp, and he felt slick, smart, tough, and good looking enough to play it. He spent time hanging around them to learn the game and develop a business agenda. It didn't take long for him to learn the trade. Robert changed his wardrobe and hair to be as stylish as the pimps and players he envied.

One particular hooker named Josie gave him special attention each time she saw him, and Robert capitalized on that. Josie had told Robert's sister that she thought Robert was cute, and that started rumors that a hooker

28

was interested in him. He, however, saw the situation as a business opportunity. He asked her to meet him at the poolroom one Friday at 7:00 p.m. He wasn't sure if she would show up, but she did, and she was dressed to kill. Everyone gawked at her as she walked in. She scanned the room, looking for him. He sat in the corner of the smoky, dimly lit poolroom. She spied him, and her smile brightened up the room. They greeted each other and discussed business opportunities. Robert was after one thing—making more money through her; he wasn't interested in dating her. After the business meeting, his drive to play the game of a pimp became his obsession. In the meantime, his father's life was fading.

Alcoholism: The Disease That Stole His Father

Robert loved spending time with his father, but he didn't like his father's alcoholism. His father neglected his responsibilities at home and disrespected his wife. He remembers the arguments his father had with his wife about not coming home after work. Many times, he would spend his paycheck at bars. When Robert would see him, he was so drunk that he could barely function. Robert would drive his father from bar to bar to keep him from getting behind the wheel. His father neglected to pay his bills plenty of times; Robert remembers that the electricity and gas were turned off twice while he was living with him.

Robert saw what alcoholism had done to his father and felt sorry for him because he knew he was suffering from alcohol abuse and had no control over it. He watched the dreaded disease consume his father's life; he ultimately died of sclerosis of the liver. Robert remembers wondering,

Did he drink because it wasn't going to change his fatal outcome? Or did he drink because he had no control over the alcohol? He will never know the answer to either question. Robert understood the danger of substance abuse and how it could kill those who couldn't manage it. After seeing the damaging effects of alcoholism firsthand, Robert vowed never to let a substance control him or cloud his judgment. "All people should fear any type of substance that can control their lives even unto death," he said.

Anger and Relationships

Robert still didn't quite understand that anger had consequences as well. His anger affected his family, friends, associates, and all the wonderful people in his life. He didn't realize how destructive his teenage anger was until he experienced the consequences of his actions. Slowly but surely, he started to push away the people close to him. His family put up with him because they understood his personal struggles. His brother, sisters, and he shared the same thoughts about his mother's controlling ways. This common bond of understanding kept the Harris kids close. They all experienced the anger and resentment, which affected them differently in their adult lives.

One morning, Robert's mother whipped him for disrupting her sleep. He was so frustrated that he wanted to fight anyone who said anything to him—one word, and they'd get a "beat down" as he called it. He wore anger like a mask and carried his bad attitude everywhere he went. Everyone notice it. One of his woman friends always asked him, "Why are you so mean to people?" He didn't understand why she always asked him that; he didn't think anything was wrong with himself.

Later in Robert's adult years, he began to see the effect his mother's abuse had had on his relationships. Her strict ways during his childhood led to anger issues in his teenage and adult years. The feedback he received in those relationships helped him to gain insight about himself; he had not realized his need to change his attitude and deal with his anger. He said, "I knew I had to make changes to become a better person." He was challenged by his thinking that led him to believe nothing was wrong with him.

When Robert was ready to indulge in a relationship, his anger came out at all the wrong times, and it was difficult to control. He slowly began to see the repercussions of his bad attitude and the impact on his relationships with family, friends, and women. As a young adult, he began to make the connection between his mother's abuse and control and his anger and aggression issues. For years, he resented his mother's hard and unbearable ways. He hated how she took away some of the best years of his life by not allowing him to be a normal teenager and forcing hard-core religion on him.

His aggressive behavior surfaced in his first serious relationship. Robert met a young woman he fell in love with. He knew it was love because of the way he felt. He thought she was beautiful and smart and had a lot going for her. They came from very different backgrounds; she lived in a middle-class neighborhood, and the two-year age difference between them was significant at his young age. But it didn't matter; they were in love.

After six months, however, he started noticing that she looked at other guys. He thought she was attracted to them even though she never indicated she was. At the time, he didn't realize that looking at other guys or people was normal. His negative thinking began to emerge as an insecurity he didn't learn to control. He dwelled on bad thoughts and began to interpret them as problems his women friends had, not him. He wondered what was wrong with the way he looked; he had thought he was very handsome. She had never complained about his looks, but he felt insecure when he felt she was looking at other men.

He finally asked her, "Why are you always looking at other dudes when we're hanging out?" She responded, "I don't know what you're talking about." They began to have arguments about looking at other guys and little things that really didn't matter. This was the beginning of his insecurities surfacing in his relationships with women, and things went downhill from there. Whenever they were out together, he would always get this funny feeling in his stomach that he had no control over when she looked at other men or when he thought she was. He started acting out in a very controlling and domineering manner because he didn't know how to deal with his low self-esteem.

The Effects of Abuse on Family

Robert's mother had affected all the Harris kids with the abuse and control she exercised over them. Robert remembers that his youngest sister was visiting a friend across the street from a park where her son was playing. She kept an eye on him, but in less than a few minutes, he ventured away from the park. She panicked. She ran to the park, screaming his name and looking for him, but she couldn't locate him. Afraid and upset, she reached out to neighbors and friends before calling the police. Not long after he went missing, a stranger returned him to her home. Robert's sister was relieved to see her son, but she was afraid and very angry as well that he had left the park. She yelled at him, and he started to cry uncontrollably. "Why did you leave the park when I told you not to?" she demanded. He didn't know what to expect, but Robert did. She whipped her son for his disobedience. Robert, who was there, flashed back to the whippings their mother had given them. He got between her and his nephew and spoke to his sister. "Stop! What are you doing?" "He should have known better than to leave the park," she said.

His sister had a temper too; lack of emotional control was a family tradition. He explained to his sister that their mother used to do the same thing to them and it had made them feel bad and angry. He asked, "Why are you doing the same thing to your son? It's not going to make him feel better or solve the problem. Whipping him is not the way to address the problem. You need to talk to him gently so he'll listen and obey you in the future." He warned her of the lasting effects of abuse and that she had to stop and consider how she was repeating the pattern their mother had established.

She thought about what he said, but she justified the whipping because the abuse from her childhood was ingrained in her. Robert understood, but he didn't like the concept of negative behaviors being transferred from one generation to another. He realized that some of his siblings hadn't learned from their experience and had suffered the consequences of their actions. If no one else in his family understood, he did. He knew that change had to begin with him.

CHAPTER FOUR

Conquering His Anger and Control and Living as a Free Man

As an adult away from home and living his own life, Robert came to understand better his mother's way of thinking even though he didn't agree with it. He realized his anger wouldn't change the past and could harm his future. He thought about becoming a better person. Reflecting on the past, obtaining feedback from people in his life, and seeing the consequences of his behavior helped him take charge of his life. He took a hard look at himself and knew he had to change his thinking. He also reflected on the spiritual component of his life that was missing. He remembers his mother telling him to read Psalm 23:1–6 (KJV) every day and to keep it with him everywhere he went.

> The LORD is my shepherd; I shall not want. He maketh me to lie down in green pastures: he leadeth me beside the still waters. He restoreth my soul: he leadeth me in the paths of righteousness for his name's sake. Yea, though I walk through the valley of the shadow of death, I will fear no evil: for thou art with me; thy rod and thy staff they comfort me. Thou preparest a table before me in the presence of mine enemies: thou

anointest my head with oil; my cup runneth over. Surely goodness and mercy shall follow me all the days of my life: and I will dwell in the house of the LORD forever.

In addition to the Psalms, Robert read the Bible every day as his mother had suggested, and his thinking began to change. He wanted to transform himself, and he believed he could in Jesus Christ. He was familiar with 2 Corinthians 5:17 (KJV): "Therefore if any man be in Christ, he is a new creature: old things are passed away; behold all things are become new."

At times, he still struggles with negative thinking. But he addresses those thoughts by praying, studying Scripture, focusing on positive things, surrounding himself with positive people, and staying connected with a church that develops people based on biblical principles. He found that these principles worked positively for him. However, he began to understand that patience and persistence was part of his personal change process.

His Insecurities Unmasked

Even after his spiritual awakening, Robert still dealt with anger issues. Though Robert weighed only 125 pounds, his quick temper caused him to aggressively confront anyone who challenged his manhood. His anger continued to affect his relationships with the woman in his life at the time. His thinking about their relationship was unhealthy; he was domineering and controlling and wanted to know her whereabouts at all times because of his suspicions, not because of anything she had done. He wanted to know what men she had spoken to any one day. He was very insecure in this relationship as well as others because of his trust issues that stemmed from being a player in his young adult life. He did what he wanted to do when he felt like it; he felt women should feel privileged to be with him, not the other way around.

He gave into his negative thoughts and behaviors, and as a result, his past attitude and careless ways haunted his relationships, which he managed through control, domination, and meanness. As a result, no matter how sweet his relationships started, they all turned sour. This just aggravated his worst behaviors; he didn't see that his ways were abusive or harmful to his woman or their relationship.

He started reflecting on the feedback he received from the women he was involved with because he had a difficult time keeping them in his life. It was no problem for him to get them; keeping them was. He wondered if they were really meant to stay in his life, but he knew there was no excuse for his unhealthy thinking and actions. It was his wakeup call to do something about himself. For the first time, conviction took place in him. He was troubled about his ways and realized he had to fix them and stop pushing good people away by refusing to let negative thoughts about the past rule him.

Failed Marriages: A Sign of His Bad Behavior

Robert went through two unsuccessful marriages that caused him hurt and pain, especially because there were kids in involved. His negative attitude prevented him from being a responsible family man. It didn't allow him to be loving, kind, forgiving, and open-minded toward his wives. At the heart of his negative thinking was pride; he had plenty of that, and he allowed it to rule him more often than not. He thought that his ways were right and that he should not be challenged. He had very little respect for his wives or any woman in his life because he was not open-minded and thought their thinking was secondary to his. This led him to believe that no relationship would last. His negative thinking and bad behaviors led only to arguments, tension, and disrespect. Discussions always escalated into a shouting match and words said that could not be taken back. After a while, Robert and those he was involved with had no respect for each other.

His street mentality affected his relationships because the people in his circle possessed the same mentality. He never liked to be challenged and was always suspicious of people no matter who they were. He realized that this was not taking charge. Rules and values of the street had a grip on him, and he introduced street mentality into his relationships for no good reason. It was hard to break such mental habits because he had lived by that code for years; he didn't know how to be loving and affectionate to the women in his life. His way was the right way, which meant he frequently didn't compromise or listen to his partner.

His first wife tried to communicate with him about his behavior, but he was defensive and justified his actions. He felt his manhood was threatened. For instance, he had conversations with his wife that escalated into arguments and disrespect. He said, "We talked, but we failed to listen and find a resolution." At the time, she told him, "You will never be in a successful relationship unless you change your ways." He bluntly told her, "I'll always have someone in my life and will never be alone." However, he failed to realize that lasting relationships were based on keeping others in your life through love, care, respect, and much more. He still didn't understand that getting a woman was different from keeping one.

After five years and two children, the relationship ended. He reached a low in his life and found himself on the streets with nowhere to go. He slept on his job for two nights and thought about what had happened. He never accepted any blame for his failed marriage; all he could think about was how wrong his wife had been. He was in such denial that he used to say that his wife was going to want him back but he wouldn't be there. Reality hit him hard when she didn't call. His immaturity and stubbornness led him to a place of loss and loneliness. In reality, he had lost his wife. He became angry with himself because two innocent kids were involved, but rather than trying to make things right, he allowed his pride to get in the way. He considered resolution to be a sign of weakness, and his sense of his manhood didn't allow him to ever seem weak. He always wanted his woman to respect him and know she had a committed man in her life.

As time passed, however, he learned that respect had to be earned. His negative thinking prevented him from putting things in proper perspective in his relationships; his ways were selfish, closed minded, and unproductive, thus, he was never able to resolve relationship issues. He used to undermine his partner's way of thinking by dominating the conversations and not listening to what she had to say. Everyone but he seemed to know he had a bad attitude. But facing the consequences of his bad behaviors in relationships finally led him to think about becoming a better person.

The Beginning of Change: Second Marriage

Even though his second marriage ended in pain and disappointment, Robert was blessed to have another daughter. The relationship had good moments. For instance, his second wife was highly motivated and obtained her bachelor's and master's degrees early in their marriage. Education was very important to her, and he admired her passion to achieve academic success. At the time, he was working dead-end jobs that provided him with little motivation and no opportunity for growth. He constantly complained about them, and it became a source of stress in their relationship. His wife convinced him to think about his options and do something to achieve them instead of complaining. He spoke to management about advancing in his work, and he learned he needed a degree or to take courses through the union to advance. He wasn't surprised; he knew he had to go back to school if he wanted any promotions, more pay, and better opportunities. He spoke to his wife about management's response, and she responded with her support. She looked for an educational program that fit his needs. She saw a Technical Career Institute (TCI) College of Technology ad that offered a program that would provide him with the skills he needed to get ahead without being in school for a long time. He was worried about the cost of the program, but his wife encouraged him to speak with a representative. He did, and he took a skills test he did very well on. That was all the inspiration he needed to start working on a degree.

Robert started classes and obtained certificates for completing his course work. In 2003, he obtained an associate's degree in building maintenance technology. His self-confidence increased as doors of opportunity opened. He started to feel blessed even though he had plenty of tough times. He finally obtained a job in his field of study. He is thankful and says, "I am blessed to have had a good job for more than eight years. Through it all,

God continued to remain faithful even though my attitude wasn't always the best. I'm grateful that God's love for me isn't contingent upon my attitudes and ways. His love makes me strive to be better at all I do regardless of my past failures."

Being a Better Man: Putting God First in His Life

Robert found it difficult to see that his attitude was a large part of his problems. Reflecting is a resourceful tool for reality checks and getting an understanding of past mistakes. He grew up living a hard life and constantly seeing black men as pimps and drug dealers and black women as prostitutes every time he stepped outside his door into the projects' familiar surroundings of false promises and the lack of hope. He associated the cars, women, clothes, hardness, bling, and slickness with success. It is what he could relate to growing up in the projects, not clean-cut white men in suits and ties carrying briefcases. His bad attitude was a means of survival, and its consequences were far reaching. It wasn't until after receiving feedback and times alone that he asked himself, *What did I do wrong? I have to change to be a better person and a good man in a relationship.*

He thought about the feedback he had received about his aggressiveness, meanness, and control from a number of people. After a while, he realized that not everyone who told him he had a problem was wrong. In order to find peace and solitude, he prayed, studied the Scriptures, and joined a solid church for his personal growth. He tried God; he figured he had nothing to lose. He began to read the Bible and pray daily. His hunger for a deeper relationship in Christ increased. Romans 10:13 (KJV) reads, "For whosoever shall call upon the name of the Lord shall be saved." He earnestly called upon the name of the Lord over time, and God heard him and began answering his prayers, which allowed his faith to grow. For the first time, he had hope. He didn't understand it all, but he did understand that his life had a purpose, and that helped him look at people differently. He displayed acts of kindness, respect, open-mindedness, and encouragement.

He started believing in what his mother taught him about God's Word and the church. Her words finally made sense to him and no longer haunted him with conviction. As a teenager, he hadn't been interested in going to church; that interfered with his livelihood. However, when he became an adult, her beliefs and values became important to him. He had faith and believed in his prayers and the Word of God. He found a church that inspired him to develop a relationship with Jesus Christ and knew that personal change would follow.

With time, persistence, teachings, and faith in the Lord Jesus Christ, he became a better man. Robert believes he is a work in progress: "I thank God for who I am today." He continues to reflect on Jeremiah 29:11 (KJV): "For I know the thoughts that I think toward you, saith the LORD, thoughts of peace, and not of evil, to give you an expected end."

Robert has learned what it takes to make a relationship work. First, he believes that changing negative thoughts is a process that requires him to improve his lifestyle for the better. Better behaviors are a result of changed thinking. He focuses on positive things more and more and studies

Scripture daily to ensure that his thinking is sound and full of hope. When he is challenged, the Word of God helps him overcome negative thoughts rather than give in to them. Romans 12:2 (KJV) states, "And be not conformed to this world: but be ye transformed by the renewing of your mind, that ye may prove what [is] that good, and acceptable, and perfect, will of God."

He believes that relationships require selflessness and respect, thinking of your partner more than you think of yourself. He feels that being on the same page and sharing innermost thoughts without judging the other person is best fostered by consistent and healthy communication. He believes that problems should not be allowed to escalate, that both parties should seek resolutions to them.

He also believes that relationships need to be managed with care by two people because relationships don't operate on their own. Finally, he believes that it is important to forgive and move forward. Robert said, "Forgiveness is not a license to continue to do wrong." Ephesians 4:32 (KJV) states, "And be ye kind one to another, tenderhearted, forgiving one another, even as God for Christ's sake hath forgiven you." He understands that it takes a mature person to do what is right without making excuses simply because he loves his partner. He understands that there are many important aspects of a relationship to manage but that the most important part of the relationship is putting God first. There is no cost to trying Him.

Robert said, "If you both put God first, your relationship will progress." Robert wonders where he would be today without God as the center of his life. He is grateful that God gave him a second chance to become a better person.

God continues to show him how to love, respect, and be kind, and God's great patience for Robert has taught him how to be patient in return.

Today, he has a beautiful woman he loves very much, and she is very supportive of him. They cherish God as the center of their life. He says, "My lovely lady is my champion because she's taught me to love her, myself, and life in general."

Robert believes that all he experienced early in life occurred because of two main reasons: he didn't have his father to give him the direction and guidance he needed, and his mother told him what not to do rather than focusing on the wonderful things he could do. His mother had done what she thought was right. She struggled financially and had a hard life as a single mother with five children trying to make it without his father's help. Robert was just a poor black boy growing up in the South trying to survive. But God had a purpose for his life; because of God's love for him, he is today a man striving to better myself and willing to share his story of truth with others, especially men looking for answers about how to deal with their insecurities. He encourages men to discuss and address their insecurities with their partners to become better people, husbands, partners, and family men.

Today, Robert loves the man he has become. Each morning, he wakes up feeling good because God didn't give up on him. Rather, God pursued him and let him know he could have a wonderful life in spite of his past. His past does not dictate who he is today because God said he was a new creature in Him with a purpose and destiny.

He currently shares the gospel with people daily, and he is not ashamed to say, "I serve a good and loving God who gives me daily direction and hope for my life." Romans 8:28 (KJV) states, "And we know that all things work together for good to them that love God, to them who are the called according to His purpose."

God has blessed Robert with four wonderful kids he loves very much; every day, he thanks God for them and the new life he is living.

PART II

Seven Deep
Insecurities of Men

CHAPTER ONE

Negative Thoughts

The early discussions on relationships began with my partner one Friday morning in the spring of 2012 in the car on my way to work in New York. As a woman, I was interested in a man's firsthand perspective on relationships. I simply wanted to know what successful strategies men have used to pursue women of interest. I asked my partner about that and hoped he would answer in all honesty. He candidly and confidently stated that a man could get any woman he wanted if he used the right strategies. That response aroused my curiosity. I thought, *If one man thinks this way, how do others think?*

My curiosity led me to ask more questions and engage in deeper discussions. Many women want to know what men think about them in light of relationships, and I was definitely one of those women. The more questions I asked, the more my partner willingly answered each question with wisdom, confidence, understanding, and honesty.

After several discussions, I concluded that it would be great to share our thoughts and insights about successful relationship strategies as well as research from other sources. I began informative discussions with male friends and colleagues and discovered that men share deep, dark secrets about women and relationships they do not want them to know about—in particular, their own insecurities. Discussion outcomes led us to develop a survey for men about some of their most secretive thoughts on relationships.

To better understand men's perceptions about relationships, I administered a survey to five thousand men between the ages of eighteen and fifty-five. Over 40 percent of the men who responded chose "negative thoughts" as their first insecurity in a relationship. Over 75 percent addressed their negative thoughts with their partners, while 45 percent chose communication as their first-choice solution for addressing negative thoughts with their partners. Over 22 percent of those men used self-help resources followed by couple's counseling, individual counseling, or other remedies. Negative thinking prevents relationships from healthy progress (Temple 2009). To provide further insight, we conducted interviews with males to capture more information on their perceptions of their insecurities.

Lingering Thoughts from the Past

Thinking has a great deal to do with the type of behavior individuals exhibit when addressing problems; this also applies to relationships. Individuals often reflect on the past, which could be positive or negative, when they address problems. If negative thoughts of the past govern their thinking, more than likely, they will affect how they manage problems. Negative thinking and behaviors rarely lend themselves to positive outcomes.

Interviewees identified "lingering thoughts from the past" as a key challenge men deal with daily in their personal lives as well as in relationships. Past thoughts described ranged from childhood problems to unhealthy relationships. These problems can include abuse, lack of love, control, temper tantrums, accusing, provoking, lack of respect, and others.

The Personal Battle with Lingering Thoughts

Couples often reflect on negative memories when they attempt to resolve problems in their relationships. These thoughts are often introduced early in relationships without the couple realizing it. As a result, negative thoughts can lead to poor communication, finger pointing, blaming, distancing, and lack of respect. These behaviors often create bad feelings that can lead to mistrust, cheating, carelessness, and possibly separation. Lingering thoughts can cloud judgment and decision making that can negatively affect relationships if they are not dealt with. They can keep people trapped in the past and prevent them from moving forward. Many couples are held captive by their thoughts of the past and don't realize they have accepted and adopted these thoughts as principles that govern their relationships; they can thus fall prey to unhealthy thinking patterns.

The following story is a scenario based on characteristics shared by a number of men surveyed. One young man who had been married for two years really loved his wife, but he had a very aggressive nature when it came to handling problems, and this often led to arguments and mistrust. His aggression stemmed from a difficult childhood; he used aggression as a means to take control of situations without considering others. He constantly used aggression when dealing with his wife and failed to see the damage it caused until it was too late.

His aggression contributed to his insecurities that existed for many years. It made matters worse when he caught his fiancée cheating on him.

The couple was not successful in resolving their problems for many reasons, including aggression, disrespect, mistrust, lack of the ability to forgive, blaming, and arguments that escalated out of control. They were no longer on the same page, and they lacked the maturity and knowledge to save their relationship. Yet they loved each other very much. The young man knew he had to change his way of thinking if he wanted a long-term, healthy relationship. He made a sincere effort to change his negative behavior. After months and years of personal work, he feels he is in a better position to contribute to a positive relationship.

He entered a new relationship with care and thought. Even though he is a much better man, he still has negative thoughts from the past, especially about cheating. He often faced fear. He almost allowed his fears of past failures to dictate his current relationship. He was willing to let go of a potentially great relationship without giving it a fair try until he had a number of heartfelt discussions with his partner. Resolution for both of them was important. The couple was able to move forward by discussing their concerns openly without assumptions and accusations. The young man was challenged by the difficulty in understanding the difference between past thoughts and legitimate questions regarding his current relationship. He joked with his partner about her "imaginary boyfriend" when he thought she was not honest about her whereabouts. At first, she ignored the joking. It didn't take long for her to become defensive toward him whenever he assumed that she wasn't honest. The accusations created tension in their relationship. At that point, he realized he had to take control of his negative thinking because it was affecting how he felt about his partner. He knew that eradicating unwarranted thoughts altogether was the key to moving forward in the relationship. He continued to make every effort to be on the same page and communicate honestly with his partner about everything important in their relationship.

Talking about issues without assumptions or accusations prevents escalation and allows for healthy dialogue. Otherwise, trust becomes an issue no matter how much two people communicate. Negative thinking can hinder personal growth as well as relationships. Therefore, recognize the warning signs and incorporate strategies to address them.

Recognize the Warning Signs of Negative Thinking

Dwelling on negative thoughts is a sign that you should change your thinking. First, negative thoughts can create stress, which can cause fatigue, difficulty in thinking, headaches, irritability, and sleeplessness. According to Mind Tools (2012), stress is a result of how an individual perceives a problem. Stress should be managed by you and your partner for your mutual benefit.

Second, negative thoughts can also lead to pessimism in a relationship. Those who think negatively often see the glass as half empty. Pay special attention to how you address a problem with your partner. Do you and or your partner complain about problems, or do you resolve them? Finding a solution is a positive approach to addressing problems with your partner rather than complaining or trying to justify your position, which can make problems worse.

Third, negative thoughts can cause a distorted self-image, for instance, assuming you are always right when you aren't. Such thinking doesn't lend itself to healthy discussions with your partner. If your partner feels he or she is never right, this can shut down communication and foster defensiveness. Be careful with using generalities to indirectly accuse your partner of anything; your partner is much smarter than you think. Using undermining tactics that do not address the issue does not resolve the problem, especially if your partner feels you are trying to blame or accuse him or her of something.

These are only some of the outcomes of negative thinking; recognizing negative thinking early on in a relationship can help solve problems. If you can recognize negative thinking, you will be better able to create successful strategies to resolve it.

Strategies for Addressing Negative Thoughts

You can address negative thoughts in a number of ways. Develop a consistent mental workout regime to improve your thinking by sleeping better, reducing irritability, and avoiding getting fatigued. A healthy diet will lead to a healthier mental state and improved quality of life. Diet changes and a consistent workout regime help you stay calmer when you're communicating with your partner about a problem; it will also help you stay focused.

Being calm and mindful of your partner is easier said than done. It takes a conscious daily effort to incorporate healthy thinking that leads to positive change. In essence, you are trying to take control of a situation in a productive and considerate manner. Therefore, your conversation will be more rational and respectful and you will address the problem directly.

Honesty about your thoughts and sharing what is important to you with your partner promotes stability in the relationship. Being honest about your feelings is not easy because pride can become an issue. However, your partner will respect you more, and that will promote a healthier bond.

Take accountability for your negative thinking by letting go of the past. Focus on positive things that matter to your relationship. Remember to examine yourself before approaching the situation with your partner. Often, the problem starts in you, so through self-examination, you will not be as quick to blame your partner for the problem.

Find a resolution for your issue that you both can agree upon and move forward. It will be one less thing to worry about; you and your partner can spend time focusing on worthwhile areas of your relationship. Positive thinking allows you to see the opportunities more clearly as well as improve skills, health and work (Clear 2013, 1).

Humility, kindness, respect, and honesty go far. Make a mental note to practice these daily. Every time you think your partner should be doing something for you, do something nice for him or her. For example, consider acts of kindness, which may include but are not limited to paying your partner compliments, being more affectionate, and providing tokens of appreciation such as flowers or an intimate date. There are simple things you can do to make your partner feel comfortable with you so he or she will return the attention and affection. Positive thinking leads to desired goals in the future (Donlan 2008), but it takes practice. Therefore, you have to decide when to make changes for the better.

By applying yourself and taking advantage of self-help resources, counseling, and open discussions with your partner, you can learn to master positive thinking and have a healthier, long-lasting relationship. The strategies mentioned here have worked in relationships and may give you a fresh perspective on yours. There is no one solution; good relationships require daily management. On that note, healthy relationships are invaluable, provide beautiful benefits, and have to be maintained by you and your partner.

CHAPTER TWO

Manhood

Men from many cultures and age groups use the word *manhood*, but they frequently define it differently. The definition of manhood continues to evolve based on differing viewpoints in society, which has led to the confusion of the male identity (Clark 2007). Societal influences include but are not limited to the emergence of feminism (Gilbert 2009), a rise in the level of education (NCES 2012) and income for women (Bureau of Labor Statistics 2010), and changing roles of men and women (Gilbert 2009). These influences may cause couples to reevaluate their relationships.

A man's behavior is also influenced by his beliefs, values, and philosophies. We can define manhood according to two basic philosophies based on feedback we received from our discussion groups. First, manhood is often referred to as a man's sexual behavior, but that definition is one-dimensional. Manhood can include a man's emotional, psychological, physical, sexual, and spiritual well-being, a multidimensional philosophy that is more representative of a man's total being and considered to be more of a holistic perception.

However, we can understand manhood based on how a man behaves in a serious relationship as governed by the unique needs of that relationship in addition to social and cultural norms. Therefore, the definition of manhood warrants the consideration of other dimensional characteristics such as how well a man manages his financial responsibilities, practices fair and equitable decision making, controls his emotional state and sexuality, and how he maintains his spiritual well-being in a relationship. Dr. Robert Lewis, founder of Men's Fraternity and founder of the Authentic Manhood website, inspired a global movement that focuses on real issues men face regarding their manhood from a spiritual perspective. The movement defines a man as someone who rejects passivity, expects the greater reward, accepts responsibility, and leads courageously (Lewis 2011).

The leadership concept Lewis raises is a societal norm that helps define a man's character. However, there are others, such as socioeconomic status, looks, notoriety, intelligence, and others that add additional meaning to the concept of manhood. Manhood encompasses dimensional aspects of a man's behavior, such as a) altruism, b) agreeableness, c) conscientiousness, d) neuroticism, and e) openness, which external and internal influences govern (Rentfrow 2009). These influences could ultimately dictate how a man will behave in a serious relationship.

Discussion groups and the survey administered to men provided further insight on the different perceptions of manhood. An important aspect of manhood that resulted from group discussions was spirituality, which can play a significant role in the lives of men but is often ignored or neglected as an aspect of manhood.

Thirty-four percent of the men who responded to the survey chose manhood as their second insecurity in a relationship. The concept of manhood challenges younger and older men as they struggle with who they are at different stages of their lives. The differences in perception confuse the definition of manhood creating identity crises for men of all ages and backgrounds.

The Personal Battle with Manhood

The shifting roles of men and women in relationships have complicated the meaning of manhood. One of the traditional definitions of manhood focuses on a man's sexual nature, but that does not define his total being in terms of how he interacts in a relationship. The definition of manhood should include how a man behaves in a relationship based on his mental, physical, and spiritual well-being. The belief that man is spiritual cannot be neglected; it is not realistic to consider a man's complete dimensional well-being without it. Manhood in its totality is closely related to the biblical definition that man comprises a body, soul, and spirit (Sanchez 2003). Subcomponents, including emotional and sexual aspects, to these dimensions should be considered.

In relation to the dimensional levels are personality characteristics that further define a man's being, such as cultural backgrounds, preferences, leadership abilities, intellect, and so forth. The best definition of manhood, especially as it relates to relationships, includes a man's complete and dynamic nature.

The following story is a scenario based on characteristics shared by a number of men surveyed. One married man thought realistically about his contributions to his marriage and what he should do to strengthen his promising long-term marriage. He had discovered that relationships were a learning process and required consistent attention through healthy and respectful communication.

In the beginning of their marriage, his values and beliefs were very traditional in terms of manhood; he believed it was his responsibility to

a) be the breadwinner;
b) make major decisions even without consulting his wife;
c) manage the finances;
d) protect his wife;
e) take charge of situations;
f) provide a stable home environment;
g) provide leadership; and
h) maintain a spiritual lifestyle that governed their home.

His values and beliefs seemed to work best early in their marriage of nine years. He tried to honor those beliefs, but it became difficult at times because his wife had her own way of thinking that he needed to take into consideration.

Over time, the couple's relationship developed other needs. He found out that the traditional role he once believed in so much did not adequately support their dynamic relationship needs due to personal, lifestyle, and financial changes. Therefore, manhood took on a slightly different meaning for him than it had when he got married. Early in their marriage, they communicated about some things. However, he did not realize that defining such expectations about his manhood had created such an imbalance in their marriage. For instance, many times, he did not discuss matters with his wife especially if he thought it caused her stress. His wife easily stressed about many things such as her family, driving, finances, and so on. He kept important decisions and family issues from her and dealt with them on his own. He thought it was his duty to protect her from external stressors as much as possible, but this was not realistic.

Later, he realized that not discussing things with her became a stressor to him. He held everything inside, and his eating habits became worse because of stress; he started eating fast-food lunches. He also began to get headaches and suffer from insomnia and stomach aches. His family had taught him that men took charge of their families as heads of their household. Therefore, other members of his family often came to him for assistance with problems, and he helped them as often as he could. He helped an alcoholic in-law who was having difficulty managing his personal affairs because he wanted to keep his wife from stressing out about it herself. Such problems outside his immediate family, however, started dominating his marriage and home life and left him stressed, tired, and irritable. The extra responsibility also created tension between his wife and him. He realized he needed to consider his priorities in light of his marriage, not his extended family.

It took some time before he began to realize that because there were two in his marriage, he had to discuss everything that could impact them in any way. It was only fair, and it did not make him less of a man. They both needed to take ownership of the relationship and marriage through equitable decision making. Keeping things to himself had not promoted his manhood; it was more of a stressor than not. But it was very difficult for him to put his manhood into proper perspective for personal experiences, thinking, values, and beliefs. He didn't recognize the flaws until they were brought to his attention. He spoke to his wife about the need for them to seek help outside of their marriage to protect what they had. He thought professional counseling would help him talk about things more openly with his wife and inspire them both to become more-active communicators.

They agreed to obtain the outside help of a reputable Christian couple who had been married for more than twenty years and were known for their success in mentoring couples. They had mentoring sessions with the couple for over six months. A few things came to light from their sessions. First, the couple discovered that relationships take commitment, communicating, respect, patience, kindness and a great deal of love and forgiveness. Second, the spiritual component of a relationship is very important to the health of that relationship. Third, a well-balanced perspective of manhood will help a man better understand what he should contribute to a relationship. Fourth, communicating with one another about all matters that may affect the relationship is important. Finally, recognizing the need for change can start someone on a beneficial journey toward self-discovery.

An increasing number of men can relate to the benefits of partnerships that include equitable decision-making processes. Men consider protecting their partners as an important aspect of their manhood. Men are challenged in this area but speak little about it because of personal experiences and beliefs. They see speaking about issues with their partners as a sign of weakness as well. Men should talk about their thoughts with their partners for their relationships to develop in a healthy way. Self-discovery and communicating based on personal experiences are beneficial and helpful to other men because the concept of manhood is complex and is perceived differently by men in relationships. It is often based on personal values and beliefs, the needs of the relationship, and their partners' needs.

Recognize Unhealthy Perspectives on Manhood

Values, beliefs, and experiences define a man's personality to a large degree. The question is whether they hinder or support his dynamic relationship (Courtright, Millar, Rogers, and Bagarozzi 1990). Just as values, beliefs, and experiences can support relationships, they can also imprison them. Therefore, it may require a man to reflect on his manhood from time to time to see if his contributions best support the needs of his relationship or marriage.

First, the lack of shared decision making in a relationship is not fair or considerate. Do you involve your partner in the decision-making process? Second, communication is important for creating shared responsibility through transparency. Do you have consistent communications with your partner about anything that may affect your relationship or marriage? Communications should include how you both feel about a matter as well as how the matter will affect your relationship.

Third, consider the stressors that impact you and your marriage. Do you address those stressors and resolve them mutually, or do you let them spiral out of control? At times, the necessity of addressing them requires the man to take the lead. Unaddressed stressors lead only to more problems that could negatively affect your relationship in the long term as well as the short term.

It may take the support and encouragement of a counselor, mentor, or self-help resources to identify and address your issues in the relationship. Incorporating strong, Christ-centered principles for spiritual growth should be among the alternatives you consider. They can be very helpful if kept in their proper perspective for addressing relationship issues holistically.

Handling Your Manhood

Understanding who you are as a man will help you put things in perspective in your relationship or marriage. Manhood is a journey of self-discovery often defined by experiences. Every man needs to evaluate who he is and change for the better each day spiritually as well as mentally and physically. The power of a consistent spiritual life with God is required for progressive change. Find a church that provides ministry to support couples as well as individuals and families. Link yourself with successful couples who have healthy relationships. Listen to how they manage the good and the bad in their relationships and consider what is applicable to yours. There is no harm in trying successful tips; they may be worth considering. However, do so with caution because every idea may not be in your best interest.

Consider manhood in light of how a man behaves in a serious relationship for more of a realistic perspective. Relationships are dynamic (Courtright, Millar, Rogers, and Bagarozzi 1990) and change based on internal and external factors. Relationships require both partners to be open-minded and considerate of each other's needs.

Don't be afraid to talk about your innermost thoughts with your partner. Men as well as women need to share their thoughts with their partners. It is fair and right, and it helps promote equality and respect in relationships.

CHAPTER THREE

Lack of Open-Mindedness

Men who are not open-minded in relationships do not consider their partner's opinions about an issue, concern, or topic equal to theirs. They fail to listen when talking and tend to value their opinions above those of their partners. Such thinking promotes miscommunication and arguments. Over 30 percent of the men who responded to the survey chose "lack of open-mindedness" as their third insecurity in relationships. Past experiences and beliefs affect many men's thoughts, attitudes, and responses about circumstances. Relationships can gauge whether men are open-minded about a situation.

The Personal Battle with a Lack of Open-Mindedness

The following story is a scenario based on characteristics shared by a number of men surveyed. One man had a wonderful relationship with his partner. He often reminisced about the first time he saw her and how beautiful she was. From time to time, whenever he saw her pass his building or cross the street, he spoke to her. He thought that if she ever gave him a chance to know her, he would be the best man she had ever had.

As time passed, he graduated to small talk with her to discover if they had similar interests, and he found out they did: action movies, traveling, amusement parks, restaurants, and more. They capitalized on those common interests as a way to get to know each other.

One day in the fall, he asked her for her number. She gave him her work number. He was not disappointed; after all, she had not said no. He considered it an opportunity to get to know her. He called her just to say hello and let her know she was on his mind. He could always picture her beautiful smile and thought he was the luckiest man alive. All he could think about was seeing her again.

They began to see each other every day for months. He knew she was the woman he would fall in love with. Today, they are deeply in love and have a beautiful relationship even though they have differences of opinions.

He can quickly analyze a situation and consider the best resolutions, while she takes her time and is very methodical in her approach and finds resolutions according to her thinking. Their driving styles differ. He feels that his driving skills are very sharp and that he's a good defensive driver. She drove the two of them a few times, and he discovered she was in need of additional skills training; he let her know that. Although she felt her driving skills were fine, she didn't deny she could improve them.

Each time she drove, he found himself coaching her on how to drive more defensively. Out of care and concern, he viewed his feedback as constructive criticism, but she became more defensive about his constant criticism as time passed. Both were stubborn; they began to debate about her ability to drive. After several months of coaching, he thought her basic skills should have improved considerably but had not. He thought she was too cautious, scared, and defensive or possibly just stubborn about learning to drive better. He never thought that her thinking patterns were the reason for the way she drove, so his supposedly constructive criticism didn't stop, and she became more defensive.

He thought about the situation to gain more understanding about their polar-opposite driving styles. Her method of driving reflected her thinking because she was very methodical and slower to act, whereas he was very reactive. Neither way of thinking was wrong; they were just different. To reduce their driving debates, they had in-depth conversations about driving from their differing perspectives, and they tried to keep open minds about the issue. They wanted to resolve the issue and not let it negatively impact their beautiful relationship any further.

She mentioned that she thought he was a bit harsh and had a tone or attitude when he criticized her. He didn't think his tone and attitude were issues; he just wanted to help her improve her skills. He was often very candid and abrupt in his criticism, which affected her sensitive nature. He often asked her to put her feelings aside and look at the bigger picture; she let him know that his criticism was anything but constructive, that it was more like constant nagging.

He began to take her concerns into consideration. After deep thought, discussion, and listening, they found a resolution. He thought it was best to refrain from the constructive criticism and provide it when necessary to relieve the tension between them. She agreed not to become defensive as long as the criticism did not occur every time she drove because it stressed her. They both made conscientious efforts to consider each other's feelings and their driving differences. They considered their differences and embraced them without allowing them to strain their relationship through expectations that may not have been realistic or fair. They learned that open communications and listening were important for resolving issues, and they learned that they thought differently and started considering each other's thoughts and opinions. They also realized that they both had to commit to the process if they wanted to progress, and they learned that patience was required in cases in which they didn't find quick resolutions. They knew they had to work together to resolve any issue. They also learned the importance of addressing issues before they spiraled out of control. Today, they talk about everything on their minds.

Open-mindedness is best for all relationships; it requires putting aside pride when discussing matters and considering differences, which could strengthen a relationship. Couples should value one another's opinions as equal partners in their relationship.

I also believe in monitoring relationships consistently for progress and growth. Instead of focusing on what open-minded is not, discuss the positive aspects of it. Find resolutions for being open-minded by recognizing the warning signs of not being open-minded and addressing them quickly as well.

Recognize the Warning Signs of Not Being Open-Minded

Being open-minded is difficult. Feedback is very important for the communication process to work. Healthy discussions can help couples be honest about issues in their relationships. There are warning signs that can help you and your partner to become more open-minded.

If you are having the same debates or arguments over one or more issues, this is a warning sign that the issue is not resolved. Continuous arguments may be because neither side is listening to the other (Turndorf 2012) or being truthful.

Couples should consider each other as equals in thoughts and opinions; this encourages respect and honesty. They should also keep in mind that their partners may not perceive things the same way, but this does not make one right or wrong. Patience is important in partners resolving any issue; that may take a number of healthy discussions and consideration of alternative resolutions to address the issue. The key is not to give up; if one discussion or resolution doesn't address the issue, quickly find another. Reflection and further discussions may be part of your resolution process. Once you have identified the warning signs, define strategies to address the issues.

Strategies for Being Open- Minded

Couples should consider successful strategies to support open-mindedness. To be open-minded, means you consider alternative thoughts about a situation in the absence of personal judgment (LaFata 2014). It's important to recognize there is an issue, to discuss the issue, and to resolve it. Creating healthy dialogue about a problem in a calm, respectful, and nonjudgmental manner is very beneficial in this process. Communicating in such a manner will keep arguments from escalating. Therefore, manage your feelings and thoughts in the communication process.

Couples should be open to each other's feedback and their thoughts on an issue; this promotes fairness in the communication process. This way, they can collectively find solutions to problems rather than trying to justify their individual positions. They both have a right to speak their minds; this will get them closer to a resolution to the problem and focus on their relationship.

It may take alternative solutions to resolve the issue. You and your partner need to stay optimistic in addressing the problem and continue to see the big picture to move forward in the right direction. It may take creative thinking from both of you to find a workable resolution. Therefore, manage your relationship and do not allow the issue to manage you. To be open-minded means to embrace each other's differences and finding solutions that work best for both of you.

CHAPTER FOUR

Low Self-Esteem

Low self-esteem is no longer a female psychological disorder; men and women suffer from it (Self Esteem Institute 2011). Men with low self-esteem present themselves as people in charge, always right, emotional, easily provoked, temperamental, and quick to blame (Ehow 2014). Such behaviors are dangerous in a relationship because men suffering from low self-esteem often seek partners with low self-esteem (Berman 2012) and often have tumultuous relationships (Sorensen 1998). Our self-esteem is formed early in childhood and can be influenced by beliefs, relationships, culture, status, religion, and experiences (Mayo Clinic 2011).

Over 30 percent of the men who responded to the survey chose "low self-esteem" as their fourth insecurity in relationships. Low self-esteem is a widespread insecurity men of all ages experience on different levels. A person's behavior can determine at what level it exists for decision making, confrontation, and life skills in general.

The Personal Battle with Low Self-Esteem

Low self-esteem is a widespread psychological problem, but many men who suffer from it don't realize they do. Low self-esteem is a man's inability to emotionally connect and often blames his inadequacies on his partner (O' Brien 2014). Ultimately, relationships can become reflections of personal weaknesses. The following story is a scenario based on characteristics shared by a number of men surveyed.

During one young man's high school days, his classmates considered him to be very popular; his male classmates were often jealous because their girlfriends showed interest in him, and he was cordial and had plenty of female friends. Indeed, he had more female than male friends. But when it came to dating long term, his low self-esteem surfaced through his attitude and behavior. Only after he had been through a number of relationships did he realize he had to change.

Early in his childhood, he had suffered emotional and physical abuse that he had never confronted. His parents never addressed the issue through counseling, so it was difficult for him to recognize it. As a child, he was very temperamental, quick to blame, and thought that he was always right. He carried that behavior into adulthood. For years, he thought that he was okay and that everyone else had problems. He thought his behavior was normal; it was part of his past family dynamics. He thought little about his behavior until his long-term relationships continued to fail.

In 2005, he was in a long-term relationship; they had been together for over four years and decided to get married in spite of their problems. They were often not on the same page about many things, such as quality of life, finances, religion and church, responsibilities, and family. But they stayed together in spite of their differences because they loved each other. He had certain beliefs and values about home life and how it should be maintained. Many of his beliefs stemmed from his family culture. He felt that if he worked, his spouse should take care of the home, cook, and do other household chores, especially if she did not work. He felt a wife had her place and should fulfill certain obligations. He felt any challenge to his values and beliefs was a sign of disrespect, and when that happened, he was temperamental and used Scripture in his defense to make his spouse respect his authority.

It worked in the beginning, but not for long. Low self-esteem makes you think you have to behave in a manner that is in reality unfair and harsh to your partner. On one occasion, the young man's spouse didn't have dinner prepared when he got home. He challenged her that day because his expectations about dinner were not met. As a result, he purposely tried to make her feel inadequate, less than a considerate spouse. His temper and tone were condescending, and his behavior created bad feelings in her. She said very little whenever he was in that mode. It took a little while before he calmed down. Once he calmed down, she told him she had had to rush her mother to the hospital because of diabetic complications that had led to a stroke. He still felt that she could have made plans to have dinner ready. He never gave his spouse the chance to explain because of his attitude, which was the beginning of her loss of respect for him.

Each time he behaved in this manner without any consideration for her point of view, a little more of the relationship was lost along with her respect. As the man of the house, he felt only his rules applied even if that meant being disrespectful to get his point across. However, it was not acceptable in his mind for his spouse to be disrespectful to him.

Much of his behavior stemmed from low self-esteem, but it took him some time before he realized that it was a major problem in his marriage. His issues caused his spouse to lose faith in him, and she ultimately left him. After the separation, he realized that their marriage had not been a partnership of shared opinions based on trust, respect, equality, and fairness. It was too late to do anything about the marriage because the emotional, psychological, and spiritual damage had been done. His wife was not willing to invest any more time in the marriage.

Low self-esteem is a poor substitute for disrespecting your partner. It is important that you recognize and address your low self-esteem by listening to your partner and taking time to look at your behaviors and see if they produce unhealthy results or responses. Once you recognize and address your problem, you can address how it affects your relationship and make personal changes. Change begins with recognizing the warning signs of low self-esteem.

Recognize the Warning Signs of Low Self-Esteem

Self-esteem is how you think and feel about yourself; it will define how you interact with your partner and others. There are few key warning signs to consider in addressing low self-esteem. First, do you belittle your partner? Is it on a consistent basis? A healthy individual does not belittle a partner to make himself or herself feel better; respect works both ways in relationships. Second, do you value or ignore your partner's thoughts and feelings? Low self-esteem is an issue that will allow you to place your thoughts and feelings above your partner's and others at all costs. You might often justify your negative behavior and consider everyone else to be wrong no matter what. Finally, how do you really feel about yourself? If you are not happy with yourself, chances are you won't make your partner happy. Once you identify the warning signs, the next step is to find strategies to address low self-esteem.

Strategies for Addressing Low Self-Esteem

The first step in addressing low self-esteem may require professional help. Low self-esteem can be a challenging and complex issue because of its possible connections to past events. In some cases, it is as simple as discussing the issues and making the changes. In others, professional help may be necessary. Here are some helpful strategies. First, a healthy relationship begins with trust and honesty, and those qualities come about when partners respect each other and listen to one another about important matters. This has to happen not just some of the time but all of the time.

Second, consider each other's feelings. Sometimes, it takes the lead of a sensitive man to understand that his partner's feelings are just as important as his. There is nothing wrong with being sensitive; it means you're in tune with yourself and possibly your partner. The next step is to make your partner or spouse feel important in a respectful manner. If your partner feels you respect him or her, you are more likely to be treated with respect in turn.

Finally, assess yourself based on how you feel and your partner's feedback. Think about your behaviors; are they negative or positive? Consider the negative behaviors and why they exist. Think about how those behaviors make you feel. Your partner's feedback may be of value. Low self-esteem can be complex and could result from issues you might need to deal with professionally such as manhood, performance issues, control, abuse, aggression, negative thinking, neglect, rejection, and many others. But always remember that it's important to talk to your partner about your feelings for your emotional and psychological health.

CHAPTER FIVE

Making Less than Your Partner

Since the Equal Pay Act of 1963 and Title VII of the Civil Rights Act of 1964, women have earned higher salaries based on education, profession, length of service, and other factors. In spite of still-existing earning disparities between men and women, an increasing number of women are the sole source of income (Center for American Progress 2013). "Almost a third of working women nationwide now out-earn their husbands" (Hartwell-Walker 2012). Their incomes have increased as they have shifted from the traditional role of stay-at-home mothers to the role of workers outside the home. Their new financial independence means they have greater input in deciding how finances will be managed in their relationships. This new dynamic of women being breadwinners can present a challenge to men. In addition to the role changes regarding income, women and men have different ways of managing their finances as well as different perceptions on making less than their partners (Ramsey 2005), and this can lead to tensions in relationships.

Nearly 30 percent of the men surveyed chose "making less than your partner" as their fifth insecurity in relationships. Men making less than their partners often resent their spouses (Mama's Health 2012). Defining expectations about finances is another challenge many couples face in their relationships, especially with the increasing number of women making more money than men or being the sole source of income.

The Personal Battle with Making Less than Your Partner

The following story is a scenario based on characteristics shared by a number of men surveyed. When one couple married fifteen years ago, their combined income was $60,000 a year; they knew little about managing finances, but they decided to start financial planning early in their marriage. They sought counseling from their pastor through several sessions, which helped a bit, but they knew they needed more help preparing for future financial challenges regarding debt management, budgeting, spending, and saving as well as their different opinions about money matters in general. Looking back, they thought they should have focused more on communicating, budgeting, saving, and planning more consistently.

Early in their marriage, the two planned on being successful, as most couples do. However, their thinking in terms of achieving success was very different; his wife thrived on educational attainment while he didn't. She focused on training and education for more than ten years of their marriage, while he considered other money-making options such as a part-time business of some sort. Even though they didn't have a written plan, they developed a budget and stuck to it as much as possible for the first few years. It was challenging. However, they were able to improve their quality of life and save a little as her income increased after three years. In addition to his full-time position, he took on a part-time job to contribute to their savings. His wife continued with her education and obtained a master's degree and is currently working on a PhD in psychology to teach and conduct research. Even though they had a little more income, they sacrificed their time together to improve their lifestyle.

Their roles shifted once she pursued a master's. He took on more of the household responsibilities while working. She continued with her studies and full-time work and helped whenever she could. They set some expectations around finances to save some and not spend frivolously. They agreed that the one with the most income would cover a larger share of the expenses. He liked to spend money on holidays, special occasions, and vacations and was not willing to forgo his traditional values. At times, he spent too much and had to borrow from her. His overspending created tension and disagreements about finances. His wife thought he was being careless and not considering their financial needs and goals. She often thought it would have been better if he covered his expenses than spend money on gifts and have to borrow from her. It was her pet peeve to say the least because it wasn't responsible money management.

The differences in thinking continued to create tension. He often thought that it was their money, not hers or his. He felt that if he worked every day, he should be able to have some freedom in spending on what he wanted to on occasion. The challenge was not that he made less but that they did not agree on how to manage their finances consistently. They did not discuss each other's thoughts about financial concerns calmly to prevent pent-up emotions and escalation of money discussions.

On one occasion, he lost his job, and she had to carry household expenses for both of them, which created greater strain on their marriage. His attitude didn't help. He often complained about not having money as he looked for a lucrative job. However, she focused on what had to be done to move forward, and she stayed positive. His circumstances made her feel as though she needed to take greater control of the finances. He often felt that she made decisions regarding finances without him because she was making more money. No matter how often they talked, they still had difficulty defining their financial expectations.

By 2012, his spouse made over $40,000 more than he did. She took on more financial responsibilities because of her income change. They also saved more. Although his income increased, it helped very little. He became depressed and sometimes resentful of the fact that he was making less than she was and thus had less control over their finances. They were on a different page when it came to spending much of the time. He had had no idea until then that making less than his spouse was a personal insecurity he needed to address. Looking back, he realized there were things they could have done to make managing their finances less challenging for both of them. He had had less than a positive attitude and could have handled things in a more mature manner.

Recognizing some of the warning signs of financial tension is important, especially because it's a key stressor in many relationships.

Recognize the Warning Signs of Financial Tension

Financial tension comes with a number of warning signs. Here are a few of the key ones. Asking and answering basic financial questions can help couples take charge of their financial futures more wisely. Future plans should include financial planning. Have you and your partner discussed your finances? If you haven't, you may be setting yourselves up for future failure, especially if you are not on the same page about the future. You need to know each other's thoughts about the future you plan to share. These thoughts should include information regarding debt as well as income. The goal is to address all financial matters, including debt, to minimize financial failure (Dhawan 2012).

Have you and your partner created realistic short-term and long-term financial goals as well as a realistic budget? It is very difficult to achieve financial success without measures in place to monitor, discuss, and tweak your goals consistently. Do you and your partner know how to manage your finances? Many couples do not have the knowledge to define financial strategies that will work in their best interest. If you both have difficulty doing so, seek reliable help in learning how to do that.

Is making less than your partner a challenge for you? If so, don't avoid the issue. Not communicating with your partner about this can cause greater tension and future financial issues, which can become stressors in other areas of your relationship. After recognizing some of the warning signs of financial tension, find successful financial strategies to address them.

Strategies for Managing Your Money Together

Take every opportunity to protect the future of your relationship by managing your finances together through open communication, planning, budgeting, and getting professional help as necessary. However, this is not a one-time deal. As lifestyles and incomes change, your financial plans should be reevaluated and revised to support your short- and long-term goals.

Make managing your finances a priority with some of these successful strategies. Through discussions, be very honest, respectful, and clear with your partner about your finances (Gehring 2012). Establish realistic financial short-term and long-term goals together (Dhawan 2012). Realistic expectations will keep you from guessing what you have to do about your finances and keep you on track regarding what is being done; it's a proactive attitude. Communicate with your partner about your financial plans as much as possible (Dhawan 2012). Keeping an open line of communications with your partner concerning finances will prevent confusion and help you manage your finances more consistently. Open communication will hold you both accountable for your finances regardless of who makes more.

If you and your partner are not savvy when it comes to managing your finances, seek reputable help and consult resources. For instance, www.About.com provides easy to follow strategies for financial planning. The site addresses topics such as debt management, savings, long-term financial planning, budgeting, and others. Another good website for couples is www.fpanet.org sponsored by the Financial Planning Association. The website provides advice, tips, and tools that can easily meet you and your partner's planning needs. CNN Money's "Money 101" (money.cnn.com/magazines/moneymag/money101/) provides an online guide to financial planning information with twenty-three topics ranging from setting priorities to 401(k)s. The "Top Ten Financial Tips" is a practical resource for couples to reference concerning their finances (Fowels 2012). Consider options that will help both of you gain financial independence together to avoid financial tension later. After all, partnerships, not "individualships," ensure successful, long-term relationships.

CHAPTER SIX

Performance Issues

Although many men deal with "performance issues," few openly discuss the topic with their partners due to embarrassment or pride. But it is difficult for men to hide their feelings from their partners, especially if they have spent significant time together.

According to WebMD (n.d.), some of the most common causes of male performance issues are physical and psychological and can range from medical conditions such as diabetes or hormonal changes to on-the-job stress, anxiety, and guilt. Performance issues for some men lead to anxiety. Men who experience anxiety over performance issues long term and do not address the issue could lose interest in sex, suffer from low self-esteem, experience problems in their relationships, and suffer from sexual dysfunction (AskMen n.d., 1). Do men of all ages, races, and cultures experience performance issues as one of their hidden insecurities?

Twenty-eight percent of the men who responded to the survey chose performance issues as their sixth area of insecurity in relationships. Even though men identified this as one of their key insecurities, they were still challenged with discussing the issue with their partners or spouses. However, it is still difficult to understand why men ranked performance issues as one of the lowest insecurities out of the seven defined, especially when it is such an important part of their manhood. Therefore, we utilized discussion groups to gain more insight from men and their perceptions on their experiences with performance issues. Their feedback included some interesting points.

- The majority of the respondents of the survey were younger than fifty.
- Stress was not a factor.
- Intimacy and sex were scheduled around their lifestyles, so the frequency of sex had decreased.
- Men were more open-minded about addressing their performance issues with a group of other men.
- Performance issues were resolved prior to the survey.

The Personal Battle with Performance Issues

Men have difficulty discussing performance issues with their partners, but it is an important topic that deserves a platform for open discussion. The following story is a scenario based on characteristics shared by a number of men surveyed.

A man and his partner were in a serious relationship for over a year prior to their marriage of two years. During their early months of dating, they spent a great deal of time together because they enjoyed each other's company very much. After six months, he became very committed. They wanted to be together long term, so they began to make plans and got married. He was sexually attracted to his wife during their marriage and wanted her all the time. She often commented that he had a high sex drive and stamina; it was easy for him to go two or three rounds in the course of a night and not feel tired. It was part of how he expressed his feelings of love and sexual attraction to her.

After the first eight months of intimacy, he began to experience problems with his performance several nights in a row. At first, he thought nothing of it. Several days passed, and he still had the issues followed by one or two good nights. After the good nights, he thought things were fine. However, the performance issues returned. He discussed it with his wife. She expressed to him that he might have been tired due to a shift change at work and possibly their financial situation.

His performance issues continued, though they seemed to improve after he had a day or two of rest. But he felt something was desperately wrong and wondered what was causing the problem. He decided to have more heartfelt discussions with his wife because his performance was affecting her as well. They reflected on what he was doing during good-performance times and thought it might be worthwhile to make changes. He decided to resume his workout schedule several times a week, watch his diet, and get adequate rest. He also thought it might help to focus on positive things more.

During their discussions about his performance issues, he and his wife focused on what had changed in their lives. Their finances had been challenging, and he felt his inflexible job schedule was stressful. These were stressors he had not dealt with before they were married. They decided it would be helpful to think about ways they could address his performance issues. They were generally intimate during the week after they got home from work, which was after nine o'clock. They considered different times, such as early mornings or right before work. Their focus was spending meaningful time together. They thought intimacy after a day or two of rest may help increase anticipation and reduce any feelings of pressure.

They didn't realize how much the lack of rest could affect his performance in spite of his being fit. In addition to rest, they realized that mental aspects impact the physical in terms of performance as well. He noticed that rest helped improve his performance. To make sure that he received rest, weekends were less structured and more relaxing whenever possible.

Intimacy does not have to mean penetration. He and his wife learned that cuddling, touching, and talking can be very satisfying way of being intimate. In addition, he learned that talking about his performance issues with his wife gave him a since of comfort; he knew he could share his insecurity without being judged. Her calmness, care, and concern gave him the confidence to be open and honest about his issue. As a result, he realized anything of importance to their relationship was worth discussing because that built trust, honesty, and intimacy.

It can be challenging to unveil your personal flaws even to your partner for fear of being judged or criticized, but it's a risk worth taking for the sake of preserving your relationship. Therefore, especially take note of warning signs and address them.

Recognize the Warning Signs of Performance Issues

When couples experience performance issues, both become aware of the issue. Therefore, it makes sense to address the issue through discussing it rather than avoiding it. However, the decision is up to you as a man to address and resolve the issue as early as possible. Identify whether you are having performance issues consistently or just very occasionally. Men can experience both issues. Therefore, it is important to understand what you are experiencing to address either appropriately.

If your performance becomes an issue, don't let pride and embarrassment keep you from addressing the problem, especially if you value your relationship. Also, it could be a health issue that warrants medical attention.

Your partner is entitled to hear from you about your problem through discussion, not attitude. Your partner deserves your honesty, consideration, and openness in discussing a very sensitive issue that affects you both.

After recognizing the warning signs, implement healthy strategies to address the issue. Please note that persistent performance issues may require professional attention. Talk to your partner about the issue out of consideration and seek the best course of action through strategies that will address your needs.

Strategies for Addressing Performance Issues

According to WebMD (n.d., 3), the best way to address performance issues is to focus on potential causes, maintain your health with the support of your doctor, reduce alcohol consumption, stop smoking, eliminate stress and anxiety as much as possible, and discuss the issue more often with your partner.

According to AskMen (n.d., 2), you can overcome anxiety by staying positive, relaxing in the confines of your comforting relationship with your partner, and taking time to cherish the beauty of your partner through intimacy. It's important for men with performance issues to acknowledge they have a problem and address it through discussions with their partners or spouses.

Once you admit that you have a performance issue, you can address the problem. As difficult as it can be to discuss it with your partner, such a discussion needs to happen because you should involve your partner in the resolution process. Healthy discussions may lead to the consideration of changes you can make concerning dieting, fitness, rest, and evaluating areas of stress in your relationship such as finances, mental or medical health issues, lack of time together, little rest, and so forth. If performance issues persist, you may need to consult a licensed professional after discussions with your partner.

Remember that intimacy can be defined only by you and your partner. Spend more quality time together by cuddling, talking, and touching as another form of intimacy. It could be as simple as spending more time relaxing with the one you love.

CHAPTER SEVEN

Pride

Men have defined "pride" as another insecurity that challenges them and their relationships. Over 25 percent of the men who responded to the survey chose "pride" as their seventh insecurity. Interviewees identified the "I am right and you are wrong" attitude as another key challenge when dealing with pride. Based on the feedback we received, men who embrace pride often deny it and do little to address it even if it becomes a problem in their relationships. Prideful men often find fault with their partners when they have difficulty addressing their personal issues, and this can lead to problems in the relationship. Pride is another form of negative thinking that can result from low or high self-esteem as well as from other personality issues.

Battling Pride and the Need to Be Right

Pride is no respecter of persons or gender, and some people frequently use it as a method of control to dominate others. Pride can give men a false sense of empowerment; it's a form of deep-seated blindness that prevents them from acknowledging their faults and causes them to find fault with their partners. Here is an example of pride and how it can distort judgment and actions in general as well as in a relationship. The following story is a scenario based on characteristics shared by a number of men surveyed.

A middle-aged man and his partner were on their way home from a vacation in Florida. At the airport, they obtained revised tickets with different seating assignments but didn't notice that until they were boarding the plane. He decided to say something to a flight attendant about the matter. He demanded that the airline correct the situation immediately; he refused to back down. The flight was completely booked and they had oversold seats, which led to the reassignment of seats. In his head, however, complaining was the right thing to do. He got louder while his partner looked at him with disbelief and embarrassment. She tried to calm him down and advised him to take his seat to prevent any more tension, but he was stubborn and refused to listen. He demanded to speak to the manager of the airlines; his fellow passengers were a captive audience. The manager boarded the airline and asked what the problem was. He stated, "This airline needs to correct our seating situation." When he requested compensation for their mishap, the manager tersely stated that the airline did not provide compensation for changed seating assignments but that he could file a complaint online. The manager told him to take his assigned seat or be escorted off the plane with his partner.

That comment caused him to get even louder. The sighs and murmurings of people on the plane continued as they waited for his performance to end. His partner continued to try to calm him down, but he still didn't listen to her. The captain of the plane told him to take his seat or leave the plane; he had already delayed the flight. As he angrily took his seat, he heard applause from the passengers around him.

His partner remained calm; he sat but still talked loudly. The captain and manager asked him to refrain from saying anything else or he and his partner would be escorted off the plane. He finally relented and kept quiet. After the plane took off, he reflected on the situation. He asked his partner for her thoughts regarding the situation. She said, "There was no need for escalating the situation in the manner you did." However, he still felt he was right.

Later on that evening, the man began to feel bad about what he had done. He and his partner talked about it. She said, "Your behavior provided little consideration for her or the others on the plane." He knew she was right. He felt awful. He apologized to her because he knew his pride had let him make a fool of himself. He had shown a lack of consideration for others but mostly for his partner.

His way of addressing the seating problem with the airline was clearly wrong. He had acted without thinking; his prideful actions were not beneficial to anyone, including himself. Additionally, he had little consideration for his partner and others. He had failed to see the big picture and that the airline provided assigned seating to get him to his destination safely. He didn't approach the matter calmly or even discuss it with his partner before taking charge. He created an unnecessary problem for both of them without considering her thoughts and feelings. As a result, both were almost escorted off the plane.

Pride is a form of dominant thinking that can govern your actions for the worse. Pride can make you feel that you're never wrong—until after the fact. Therefore, identify and address pride's warning signs.

Recognize the Warning Signs of Pride

Pride causes men to act in their best interests. It allows them to believe a situation should be handled in a certain manner regardless of their partners' feelings and often those of others. They perceive such thinking as a matter of taking charge of a situation. However, it can be a form of dominance and control used negatively to bring about a desired result that is not necessarily in the best interest of their partners or others.

Beware of the warning signs of pride. Consider your thoughts regarding a situation before acting; and consider the potential consequences. Do you take charge of a situation in the best interest of you and your partner, or are you controlling the situation with little or no consideration for your partner? Do you react before you think about the best course of action? Do you include your partner's input if necessary? Thinking about the situation before reacting is the first course of action. You should then talk with your partner about the situation before you do anything. Often, the behavior occurs before anything can be done, but it is too late then to address the problem upfront. As a result, your partner can feel that you lack consideration for him or her.

Did you not consider the big picture when thinking about resolutions? Many times, a problem is not worth taking on, especially if there is little or no positive benefit to you and your partner. It makes even less sense if individuals outside your relationship are impacted by your negative decision and behavior. The context of the matter should be considered as well. Did you approach the situation in a calm matter or with a negative attitude and tone?

Approaching a matter with a demanding attitude creates an environment of tension and can cloud your judgment. Tension makes it difficult to resolve problems and often escalates them.

These are some of the warning signs of pride that you and your partner should consider when addressing a problem. After recognizing them, find strategies that will resolve the problems as quickly as possible.

Strategies for Addressing Pride

Think before acting, especially if you and your partner can be affected negatively by your decision and behavior. The more you keep your partner in mind when it comes to addressing a situation, the easier it becomes to manage it successfully.

Discuss the issue with your partner. Collaborative decision making (Heitler 2013) can lead to greater trust between you and your partner or spouse because you are incorporating him or her upfront in the decision-making process.

Consider the big picture in dealing with problems that could affect your relationship; this will help you and your partner or spouse better understand the implications of your decisions. Sharing the decision-making process creates a sense of accountability in both of you. Act calmly when handling all problems to reduce tension, think more clearly, communicate better, be considerate of your partner's feelings, and make it easier to find a resolution. The key is to minimize any negative behavior resulting from pride by changing your thinking. The consequences of pride benefit no one.

PART III

Reflections

CHAPTER ONE

Men's Perceptions about Their Insecurities

A number of conclusions were drawn from the group discussions, survey results, and interviews we conducted regarding the perceptions of men and their insecurities. First, the values and beliefs of the men surveyed varied due to culture, experiences, choices, and age. However, men primarily shared the same insecurities based on the feedback provided.

Second, the roles of men and women continue to evolve (Gilbert 2009) and could impact how each individual contributes to a relationship. These changing roles may need to be taken into consideration when resolving issues in the relationship. Third, there appears to be a lack of healthy communications (Shimberg 1999) between couples, which could add to the complication of managing long-term relationships. Fourth, escalation of a problem or conflict occurs because a resolution is not defined and applied (Heitler 2013). Fifth, men and women think differently (McClintoch Greenberg 2012). This difference in thinking needs to be considered when discussing and addressing relationship issues to avoid misunderstandings that could escalate.

Finally, the spiritual component of a relationship is an important to couples for a healthy relationship that should not be neglected (Morin 2013). Couples who agree on the spiritual significance of marriage are better prepared for marriage, have lower divorce rates, domestic violence, invest more time in their relationship, and resolve problems through collaboration (Fagan 2006). Christian couples who are more committed when engaged in religious practices, such as attending church weekly, reading scriptures from the Bible, praying individual and together were more committed and less likely to divorce (Stanton 2011). Though emotional, psychological, physical, and social factors can influence a relationship, the spiritual component of that relationship is important, especially when couples have clear objectives for incorporating it into their relationship consistently and progressively.

Here are some strategies that men can use to address their insecurities to develop healthier relationships.

Key Strategies for Addressing Your Insecurities

To help men support and promote healthy relationships, I provide seven successful strategies to address negative thinking, manhood, not being open-minded, having low self-esteem, making less than your partner, performance issues, and pride.

Negative thinking was identified by our survey respondents as the leading insecurity. The men felt challenged more specifically by their memories. Men do not realize that unaddressed past thoughts can threaten the progress of a relationship. Therefore, the best solution for addressing negative thinking is acknowledging that it exists and eliminating it.

Pride and other insecurities can make it difficult for men to acknowledge that such a problem exists. One way to determine whether negative thinking impacts your attitude is to gauge your behavior in a relationship. Discuss your thoughts with your partner, since he or she is the closest to you and can confirm that your negative thinking is impacting your relationship. You can then find resolutions together that will positively change your thinking and behavior. After all, the relationship is about the two of you, not others.

When discussing such thoughts, you both need to be honest, respectful, and considerate of each other's feelings. Any discussions about the matter should be calm and supportive. As a man, take charge of your thinking and change for the better. Positive change begins with you.

Manhood was the second insecurity identified by men surveyed. Based on feedback, men have different perceptions of manhood according to values, beliefs, and experiences. These differences in perceptions complicate the definition of manhood and challenge the male identity (Clark 2007).

Another reason men felt challenged by their concepts of manhood was that they considered themselves spiritual as well as emotional and physical beings. Addressing one or two of those aspects of a man's being while neglecting the other or others creates an imbalance in personhood that can negatively impact a relationship. Therefore, addressing the emotional, physical, and spiritual aspects of a man is more realistic and provides more of a holistic perspective of manhood.

A man can better understand who he is by gauging his behavior in a relationship. Once again, a partner is in the best position to provide feedback on just how well a man is doing. The next step is to take responsibility and make positive changes. Self-improvement should be continuous and can better support the progress of a healthy, long-term relationship. It also inspires your partner to do the same. Therefore, you both share responsibility in managing your relationship for personal growth.

Not being open-minded was the third insecurity men felt in our survey. Being open-minded means taking your partner's thinking into consideration. Men think differently than women, and they need to consider these differences when they address issues, communicate, plan, and make decisions. Men need to understand their partners' ways of thinking.

You should first practice fair communications by being open to your partner's perspective and listening to feedback. Be humble and speak with respect. Your partner could provide insight about a situation you may not have considered. Being open-minded about your partner's thoughts promotes fairness in the communication process. You should use fair communications to find resolutions you both agree on to solve an issue. Being open-minded can help you and your partner stay focused on what really matters, seeing the big picture, and moving forward into a long-term and successful relationship.

Low self-esteem was the fourth insecurity the men identified. Low self-esteem is a negative behavior that needs to be identified and addressed. It can be complex and could result from experiences, which may require the help of a psychologist or psychiatrist to target and address the issue. However, some men have used self-help resources to address more-manageable self-esteem issues.

You should feel comfortable enough to speak with your partner about your thoughts and feelings without being criticized, blamed, or ridiculed. It is very important to talk to your partner about your feelings of low self-esteem for your emotional well-being. Start with changing your thinking to build your self-confidence. For example, discuss your feelings with your spouse or partner whenever you feel the need, engage in healthy and fun activities frequently, focus on the future but not the past, surround yourself with positive people, make sure your partner is supportive and positive, minimize complaining by maximizing positive speech, and investigate self-help resources. If need be, seek professional help as a positive step toward moving forward.

Making less than your partner was the fifth insecurity identified by the men surveyed. According to Hartell-Walker (2012), women are increasingly making higher salaries than their spouses are. Because of the shift in traditional financial roles, women have a greater stake in the decision-making process regarding financial matters. To complicate the matter, women and men manage finances in different ways (Ramsey 2005). However, salary differences do not have to present challenges.

Be proactive and find solutions to solve your financial problems together by openly discussing your financial situation, clearly defining both your financial goals, make realistic financial plans to achieve them, and consistently reevaluate your financial plans as your financial situation or lives changes. Also, seek resources and possible expert advice on money management that will best support your relationship. Helpful resources include www. About.com and www.fpanet.org for debt management, budgeting, and financial planning. CNN Money's "Money 101" (money.cnn.com/magazines/moneymag/money101/)

provides an online guide on twenty-three financial topics to assist you in lifelong planning.

Communicating consistently about financial planning (Dhawan 2012) is important to the health of your relationship because money is the number one challenge couples face in their relationships (Dr. Phil 2014). Don't be afraid to consider alternative resolutions for successfully managing money based on relationship needs.

"Performance issues" was identified as the sixth insecurity by the men surveyed. Eighty percent of the men surveyed were between ages eighteen and forty-five. Therefore, men under the age of fifty may not have experienced performance issues. If you have performance issues, discuss them with your partner before considering other alternatives. According to WebMD (n.d., 3), the best way to address performance issues is to focus on potential causes such as poor health, excessive alcohol consumption, smoking, stress, and lack of communication with partners. It may be as simple as discussing your intimacy schedule or considering changes to your diet, exercise routines, rest habits, physical and mental health, and problems with stress, and so forth. If performance issues persist after you make personal and lifestyle changes, it may be necessary for you to seek medical attention.

You and your partner are in the best position to find creative ways to improve intimacy in your relationship. Intimacy needs to be reevaluated on a consistent basis to ensure that both of you are satisfying each other willingly and passionately.

Pride was the seventh and final insecurity identified by the men surveyed. The best anecdote for pride is practicing selflessness. Being selfless is keeping your partner and others in mind regarding everything you do. Therefore, think before acting, especially if your partner and others can be affected negatively by your decision and behavior. The more you keep your partner in mind when it comes to making decisions, the easier it will be to make better decisions that will positively affect you both. Collaborative decision making can lead to greater trust between you and your partner because you are incorporating him or her upfront in the decision-making process.

At the heart of identifying the seven top insecurities of men discussed in this book is the need to resolve them through personal, positive, and progressive change. Positive personal change involves acknowledging that you have insecurities, discussing them with your partner, listening to positive and respectful feedback, and resolving those insecurities to help improve positive thinking and behaviors. We can define a man's journey of self-discovery as change that is inspiring, healthy, and continuous. Personal change promotes a healthier relationship.

CONCLUSION

Information based on research, informal discussions, blogs, websites, articles, books, related resources, and social media—to name just a few sources—provided insight on relationship issues that couples encounter today. In spite of the wealth of information, relationship issues continue to thrive among couples. Consideration should be given to more gender-specific topics to understand men and their perceptions about relationships.

The Robert Harris memoir was a case study that inspired further questions about men and their insecurities that led to focus groups, informal interviews, and surveys. As a result, the seven top insecurities defined by a group of men based on survey results add to the existing information on relationships and encourage more men to acknowledge their insecurities and do something about them. They also inspire men to have healthy discussions about their thoughts and feelings with their partners and encourage men to be more open-minded about their relationships and find successful ways to collaborate with their partners to solve relationship issues in a humble, caring, respectful, and loving manner.

Through my research, I discovered that men have different perceptions than do women regarding their roles in relationships based on individual values, beliefs, and experiences. In addition to these perceptions, societal influences and psychological, physical, and spiritual factors also complicate a man's ability to function in a healthy relationship. To help men think more earnestly about how to take charge of themselves and progress their relationships, I have developed a "Do" list for consideration and action they can refer to often.

Your "Do" List for Managing Healthy, Long-Term Relationships

1. Do remain selfless in your relationship and consider your partner in everything you do.
2. Do respect your partner through fair communication by listening as well as speaking with care.
3. Do discuss your feeling and thoughts with your partner.
4. Do listen to your partner's feedback if it can lead to positive personal change.
5. Do resolve your relationship issues through collaborative decision making.
6. Do focus on the big picture to move forward with your partner in a healthy, happy, and peaceful manner.
7. Do consider that your partner may think differently than you do and embrace those differences.
8. Do something nice for your partner often.
9. Do address the spiritual aspects of your relationship by making God the head of your lives.
10. Do keep external and internal forces from taking charge of your relationship through commitment, humility, honesty, truth, forgiveness, care, prayer, and continuous love.

This "Do" list is meant to help men focus on some of the most important action items for managing themselves in relationships. Share the list with your partner and refer to it often. The list of action items is to help you embrace positive personal change and improve your relationship. Men should focus on becoming stronger individuals first and then focusing on keeping their partners happy in the long term. Also, there is nothing wrong with seeking help in the form of counseling sooner rather than later for individual and relationship needs. Couples do not realize that relationship skills can be taught through counseling to help manage a healthy relationship long term (Meyer 2014). The art of managing a successful relationship is learning to apply the right relationship skills at the right time.

At buzzaboutrelationships.com, you can explore current relationship topics, find successful relationship strategies, find out what successful couples are doing, find relationship facts, find resources, take trivia quizzes, and make suggestions on relationship topics you would like to see covered.

BIBLIOGRAPHY

About.com. n.d. "Financial Planning." financialplan. about.com/.

AskMen. n.d. "Overcoming Performance Anxiety." www. askmen.com/dating/love_tip_60/79b_love_tip.html.

Berman, Laura. 2012. "Can Your Relationship Survive Low Self-Esteem?" www.everydayhealth.com/sexual-health/0417/can-your-relationship-survive-low-self-esteem.aspx.

Bureau of Labor Statistics. 2010. "Highlights of women's earnings in 2009." http://www.bls.gov/cps/cpswom2009.pdf.

Center for Disease Control. 2004. "Leading Causes of Death by Age Group, Black Males - United States, 2004." http://www.cdc.gov/men/lcod/2004/04black.pdf.

Center for Disease Control. 2011. "National marriage and divorce rate trends." http://www.cdc.gov/nchs/nvss/marriage_divorce_tables.htm.

Chalmers, Laura. 2014. "Federal Government Offers Newlyweds $200 Voucher to Attend Marriage Counseling." *The Courier-Mail.* http://www.couriermail.com.au/news/queensland/federal-government-offers-newlyweds-200-voucher-to-attend-marriage-counselling/story-fnihsrf2-1226808063646?nk=083a4ecc0e810392247e680e3dd01b45.

Cherry, Kenda. 2014. "The five big personality traits." http://psychology.about.com/od/personalitydevelopment/a/bigfive.htm.

Clark, Garian. 2007. "Qualities of the real Christian man."

http://www.helium.com/items/232526-qualities-of-the-real-christian-man.

Clear, James. 2013. "The science of positive thinking: How positive thoughts build

your skills, boost your health, and improve your work." *The Huffington Post.* http://www.huffingtonpost.com/james-clear/positive-thinking_b_3512202.html.

Courtright, J. A., F. E. Millar, L. E. Rogers, and D. Bagarozzi. 1990. "Interaction dynamics of relational negotiation: Reconciliation versus termination of distressed relationships." 54 (4), 429–53. DOI: 10.1080/10570319009374354. http://www.tandfonline.com/doi/pdf/10.1080/10570319009374354#.U9GrjPldWAg

CNN Money. 2013. "Money 101—Step by step guide to gaining control of your financial life." money.cnn.com/magazines/moneymag/money101/.

Dhawan, Salil. 2012. Financial planning tips for couples. www.rediff.com/getahead/slide-show/slide-show-1-money-7-financial-planning-tips-for-couples/20110802.htm

Donlan, Joseph E. 2008. "Ordaining reality." ordainingreality.com/excerpts.html.

Dr. Phil. 2014. "Money: Financial and marital harmony." *Petesky Productions, Inc.* http://www.drphil.com/articles/article/32.

Ehow. 2014. "The Signs of Low Self-Esteem in Men When Dating." www.ehow.com/info_7925410_signs-low-selfesteem-men-dating.html.

Elichmann, Jacob. 2014. "Is the average cost of marriage counseling worth it? Will it save your marriage? http://www.selfgrowth.com/articles/is-the-average-cost-of-marriage-counseling-worth-it-will-it-save-your-marriage.

Fagan, Patrick. 2006. "Why religion matters even more: The impact of religious practice on social stability." The Heritage Foundation. http://www.heritage.org/research/reports/2006/12/why-religion-matters-even-more-the-impact-of-religious-practice-on-social-stability.

Financial Planning Association. www.fpanet.org/.

Fowels, Deborah. 2012. "Top Ten Financial Tips." financialplan.about.com/cs/personalfinance/a/TopTenMoneyTips.htm.

Gehring, N. 2012. "New Couples—The First Financial Step." Financial Planning Association. www.fpanet.org/ToolsResources/TipoftheWeek/PastTips/Marriage/NewCouplesTheFirstFinancialStep/.

Gilbert, Michael. 2009. "Love, Marriage, and Darwin." Election 2012, University of Southern California. Retrieved on July 30, 2012. helection2012.usc.edu/2009/02/love-marriage-and-darwin.html.

Hartwell-Walker, Marie. 2012. "When Women Earn More Than Men." *Psych Central.* Retrieved on August 27, 2012. psychcentral.com/lib/2006/when-women-earn-more-than-men/.

Heitler, Susan. 2013. "Resolution, not conflict. What's all this talk about couples' communication skills?" *Psychology Today.* www.psychologytoday.com/blog/resolution-not-conflict/201307/whats-all-talk-about-couple-communication-skills.

Horan, Sean M. 2013. "Reasons Couples Go to Therapy." *Psychology Today.* Retrieved on July 19, 2014. http://www.psychologytoday.com/blog/adventures-in-dating/201307/reasons-couples-go-therapy.

LaFata, Alexia. 2014. "The most important quality you will ever have in your life is being open-minded." http://thoughtcatalog.com/alexia-lafata/2014/01/the-most-important-quality-you-will-ever-have-in-your-life-is-being-open-minded/.

Lee, Thomas R. n. d. "Factors that make a difference in marital success." Department of Family and Human Development, Utah State University. http://strongermarriage.org/htm/married/factors-that-make-a-difference-in-marital-success.

Lewis, Robert. 2011. "Authentic manhood." Retrieved on November 6, 2012, from http://mensfraternity.com/about/.

Madden, Mary, and Rainie, Lee. 2006. "Not looking for love: The state of romance in America." The Pew Internet & American Life Project, Pew Research Center. Retrieved on July 20, 2012. www.pewinternet.org/Reports/2006/Romance-in-America.aspx.

Mama's Health, Inc. 2012. "Women who make more money than their spouses." www.mamashealth.com/relationships/moremoney.asp.

Marriage Guardian. 2014. "What are your chances of success with marriage counseling." http://www.marriageguardian.com/success-of-marriage-counseling.html.

Mayo Clinic. 2011. "Self-esteem check: Too low, too high or just right?" www.mayoclinic.com/health/self-esteem/MH00128.

McClintoch Greenberg, Tamara. 2012. "21st century aging. Differences between men and women." *Psychology Today.* www.psychologytoday.com/blog/21st-century-aging/201209/differences-between-men-and-women.

McGuinnes, Devin. 2013. "Relationship experts share the 10 most common issues in a marriage." *Babble.* http://www.babble.com/relationships/relationship-experts-share-the-10-most-common-issues-in-a-marriage/.

Meyer, Cathy. 2014. "Benefits of marriage counseling." http://divorcesupport.about.com/od/canorshoulditbesaved/qt/marriagecounsel.htm.

MindTools. 2012. "Thought awareness, rational thinking, and positive thinking." Retrieved September 13, 2013 from www.mindtools.com/pages/article/newTCS_06.htm.

Morin, Amy. 2013. *The four main components of a healthy marriage* (blog). *The Marriage Counseling Blog*. http://marriagecounselingblog.com/marriage-co unseling/%EF%BB%BF%EF%BB%BF%EF%BB%BF the-four-main-components-of-a-healthy-marriage/.

National Center for Education Statistics. 2012. The Condition of Education 2012.

U. S. Department of Education. http://nces.ed.gov/ pubs2012/2012045.pdf.

Ottney, Sarah. 2013. "Premarital counseling helps couples prepare for marriage." Toledo Free Press. http://www. toledofreepress.com/2013/01/16/premarital-counseling-helps-couples-prepare-for-marriage/.

Ramsey, Dave. 2005. "Working with your differences."

www.focusonthefamily.com/marriage/money_and_finances/ pursuing_financial_unity/working_with_your_differences. aspx.

Rentfrow, Jason. 2009. "The Big 5 Model of Personality." *Psych Central*.

Retrieved on July 23, 2014, from

http://psychcentral.com/blog/archives/2009/11/10/the-big-5-model-of-personality/.

Sanchez, Gilbert. 2003. "The nature of man." Retrieved November 5, 2012, from http://chalcedon.edu/research/articles/?query=the++nature+of+man.

Self Esteem Institute. 2011. Questions and Answers about Low Self-Esteem (LSE). www.getesteem.com/about-self-esteem.html.

Shimberg, Elaine Fantle. 1999. Blending families. (New York: Berkley Publishing Group). www.amazon.com/Blending-Families-Elaine-Fantle-Shimberg/dp/0425166775#reader_0425166775.

Sorgen, Carol. 2012. "7 relationship problems and how to solve them." Retrieved on July 30, 2012. www.webmd.com/sex-relationships/guide/7-relationship-problems-how-solve-them (on communications and money).

Sorensen, Marilyn J. 1998. *Breaking the chain of low self-esteem.* Third edition. Portland: Wolf Publishing Co.. www.getesteem.com/books/breaking-the-chain.html.

Stanley, Howard and Markman, Howard. (2014). "Can government rescue marriages?' Center for Marital and Family Studies. University of Denver and PREP, Inc. http://www.smartmarriages.com/8.html.

Stanton, Glenn T. 2011. "Divorce rate in the church – As high as the world?" *Focus on the Family Findings.*

Focus on the Family. http://www.focusonthefamily.com/about_us/focus-findings/marriage/divorce-rate-in-the-church-as-high-as-the-world.aspx.

State of Our Unions. 2012."What is the state of marriage in America?" State of Our Unions Organization. http://www.stateofourunions.org/2012/presidents-marriage-agenda.php.

Temple, Mitch. 2009. "The marriage turnaround: How thinking differently can change everything" (Chicago: Moody Publishers). (Discusses resources for addressing issues in marriages and addresses the symptoms rather than root causes—destructive myths, thinking, and attitudes.) www.mitchtempleonline.com/page/the-marriage-turnaround.

Turndorf, Jamie. 2012. "We can work it out. Listening with your heart." *Psychology Today.* www.psychologytoday.com/blog/we-can-work-it-out/201204/listening-your-heart.

WebMD. n.d. Healthy benefits of long-term commitment.

www.webmd.com/sex-relationships/guide/relationships-marriage-and-health.

WebMD. n.d. Sexual problems in men. men.webmd.com/guide/mental-health-male-sexual-problems.

NOTES

Printed in the United States
By Bookmasters